CSR イニシアチブ

~ CSR 経営理念・行動憲章・行動基準の推奨モデル ~

[英訳付き]

CSR INITIATIVE
CSR Management Philosophy, Charter of Conduct
and Code of Conduct

水尾順一・田中宏司・清水正道・蟻生俊夫 編
馬越恵美子・昆政彦 監訳
日本経営倫理学会・CSR イニシアチブ委員会 著

日本規格協会

CSRイニシアチブの引用・転載は，著者の意向により基本的には許可いたしますが，記録等の関係上，事前に発行元である日本規格協会（普及事業部書籍出版課，TEL：03-3583-8007）までお問い合わせください．

推薦のことば

　近時のわが国企業社会において，ややブーム気味とも思えるほどに注目されているCSR（Corporate Social Responsibility：企業の社会的責任）に関して，日本経営倫理学会においても，昨春からCSR研究部会を新たに設けて本格的検討を開始した．

　本書は，同研究部会の水尾部会長を中心として，田中，清水，蟻生部会員をはじめとする20数名によるCSRイニシアチブ委員会が，このCSRの観点から経営倫理の実践のための仕組みを見直し，CSR活動の実践に役立つような基準整備を進めた結果を集大成したものである．

　そもそも企業における経営倫理の実現にとって，最も重要な基本的認識は，旧来からの効率性や競争性を重視する価値観に加えて，新しく人間性や社会性をも同等に重視する価値観への転換（シフト）と，その新しい価値観を各種ステークホルダーと共有（シェアリング）することであるといわれる．

　企業の社会的責任の必要性については既に東西の幾多の先賢が指摘してきたところであるが，今回のCSRの新味は企業のすべてのステークホルダーに対してそれぞれの固有ニーズへの適切な具体的対応を求めていることである．

　つまりCSRの実現は経営倫理学における"ステークホルダーマネジメント"に通底するものといえよう．したがって，本書は主要10大ステークホルダーごとに経営倫理の仕組みである行動憲章や行動基準の内容を整理し，法的，経済的，倫理的及び社会貢献的の四責任について，明確な具体的基準を提示しているものである．

　こうした新しい基準は，企業がこれからのCSR活動に取り組む上でステークホルダーマネジメントを実行しやすくするものである．この基準モデルを参考にして，経営倫理綱領や行動指針などを作成したり，また，見直しをしたりするのにも役立つだけでなく，CSR活動のチェック基準としても使用することができよう．最近はCSRに関する類書がかなり多い中で，本書は前記の企

業のステークホルダー対応について，定型的四責任を軸に箇条書きによる簡潔性をもって，ポイントの明確化を図った実践向きの基準書であることを特徴としている．

　企業の関係者や研究者が本書を有効に活用して，CSR活動の一層の展開と定着化を図られることを念願している次第である．

　2005年4月吉日

日本経営倫理学会
会長　水　谷　雅　一

CSR イニシアチブ委員会

代　　表：駿河台大学経済学部教授　水尾順一（兼・編集委員）
副 代 表：立教大学大学院経済学研究科教授　田中宏司（兼・編集委員）
　　　　　淑徳大学国際コミュニケーション学部教授　清水正道（兼・編集委員）
事務局長：電力中央研究所・社会経済研究所主任研究員　蟻生俊夫（兼・編集委員）
翻訳監修：桜美林大学経営政策学部教授　馬越恵美子
　　　　　ファーストリテイリング・執行役員グループ会社管理部長兼グループCSR部長
　　　　　　昆　政彦

委員（五十音順，2005年4月1日現在）

担当原稿 （ステークホルダーごと）	執　筆　委　員
消 費 者	企業社会責任フォーラム・代表／理事　阿部博人 松下電器産業・法務本部企業倫理室長　池田耕一 サントリー・コンプライアンス推進部課長　福本ともみ 駿河台大学経済学部教授　水尾順一
取 引 先	日本サプライマネジメント協会・代表取締役　上原　修 HRT　大川　恒 立教大学大学院経済学研究科教授　田中宏司
従 業 員	電力中央研究所・社会経済研究所主任研究員　蟻生俊夫 日本福祉大学客員教授　後藤芳一 前資生堂・CSR部次長　酒井　剛 ベネッセコーポレーション・常勤監査役　桜木君枝
株主・投資家	野村総合研究所・経営コンサルティング部主任コンサルタント　伊吹英子 イトーヨーカ堂　鈴木　敬 損保ジャパンリスクマネジメント・リスクコンサルティング部研究開発室部長 　　　　福田　隆
地域社会・地球環境	東京電力・総務部企業倫理グループマネージャー　小野芳幹 淑徳大学国際コミュニケーション学部教授　清水正道
競争会社	沖データ・常務取締役コンプライアンス推進委員長　橋本克彦 エーザイ・コーポレートコミュニケーション部課長　福田英男
マスメディア	ポラス・執行役員広報部長　明石雅史 日本経済新聞社・広告局業務推進部　田邊　雄
行　政	三井不動産・監査室コンプライアンスグループグループ長　佐藤伸樹 協同広告・相談役　山脇　徹 東海大学政治経済学部専任講師　横山恵子
NPO/NGO	前ノバルティスファーマ・広報マネージャー　斉藤全彦 桜美林大学経営政策学部教授　馬越恵美子 ビジネス倫理研究所・代表　山口謙吉
国際社会	東日本旅客鉄道・人事部　大泉英隆 ファーストリテイリング・執行役員グループ会社管理部長兼グループCSR部長 　　昆　政彦 駿河台大学経済学部教授　水尾順一

CSRイニシアチブ委員会事務局　[(財)電力中央研究所・社会経済研究所：事務局長　蟻生俊夫]
〒100-8126　東京都千代田区大手町1-6-1
TEL: 03-3201-6601　FAX: 03-3287-2864　E-mail: ariu@criepi.denken.or.jp

CSR INITIATIVE Committee

Representative: Junichi Mizuo, Ph.D., Professor of Business Administration, Surugadai University

Deputy-representative:
  Hiroji Tanaka, Professor, Graduate School of Economics, Rikkyo University
  Masamichi Shimizu, Professor, School of Welfare and Environment, College of Cross-Cultural Communication and Business, Shukutoku University

Secretary-general: Toshio Ariu, Senior Researcher, Socio-economic Research Center, Central Research Institute of Electric Power Industry

Translation supervision:
  Emiko Magoshi, Ph.D., Professor, College of Business and Public Administration, Obirin University
  Masahiko Kon, Executive Officer, Group Finance and Administration & Group Corporate Social Responsibility, Fast Retailing Co., Ltd.

Member (alphabetical order, as of April 1st, 2005)

"Stakeholder" category that it took charge of writing	Contributor
Consumers	Hiroto Abe, Executive Director, CSR Forum JAPAN Junichi Mizuo, Ph.D., Professor of Business Administration, Surugadai University Koichi Ikeda, General Manager, Business Ethics Office, Matsushita Electric Industrial Co., Ltd. Tomomi Fukumoto, General Manager, Compliance Department, Suntory Ltd.
Suppliers and Customers	Hiroji Tanaka, Professor, Graduate School of Economics, Rikkyo University Ko Okawa, CEO, HRT Ltd. Osamu Uehara, C.P.M. Chief Executive Officer, Institute for Supply Management Japan, Inc. TM
Employees	Kimie Sakuragi, Statutory Auditor, Benesse Corporation Toshio Ariu, Senior Researcher, Socio-economic Research Center, Central Research Institute of Electric Power Industry Tsuyoshi Sakai, Former Deputy General Manager, CSR Department, Shiseido Co., Ltd. Yoshikazu Goto, Visiting Professor, Nihon Fukushi University
Shareholders and Investors	Eiko Ibuki, Ph.D., Consultant, Management Consulting Department, Nomura Research Institute, Ltd. Takashi Fukuda, General Manager, Research & Development, Risk Consulting Department, Sompo Japan Risk Management, Inc. Takashi Suzuki, Ito-Yokado Co., Ltd.
Local Communities and Global Environment	Masamichi Shimizu, Professor, School of Welfare and Environment, College of Cross-Cultural Communication and Business, Shukutoku University Yoshimoto Ono, Manager, Business Ethics Task Force, Tokyo Electric Power Company
Competitors	Hideo Fukuda, Senior Manager, Corporate Communications Department, Eisai Co., Ltd. Katsuhiko Hashimoto, Managing Director & Chief Compliance Officer, Oki Data Corporation

まえがき

近年，CSR（Corporate Social Responsibility：企業の社会的責任）への関心が急速に高まっている．

その取組みは世界的レベルで注目され，企業の持続可能な発展の視点から企業と環境・経済・社会との共生が重要なテーマとなってきた．その背後には，世界的レベルで頻発する企業不祥事，経済のグローバル化の進展，多様な価値観をもった NGO（Non-Governmental Organization：非政府組織）の台頭，IT（Information Technology：情報技術）の発達，さらには社会や消費者の価値観の変化などがある．

これらを背景に，2004 年 6 月にストックホルムで開催された ISO（International Organization for Standardization：国際標準化機構）の国際会議で，CSR の規格化（SR 規格）が決定した．今後，世界各国で CSR への取組みが進められることとなり，日本においても経済産業省を中心に進められている．

日本経営倫理学会では，この領域に最も近い学会として，産学協同の CSR 研究部会を 2004 年 5 月から発足し，精力的に活動を進めてきた．このたび，当研究部会では，大学教授や研究者，企業人，NPO など約 30 名のメンバーで構成される"CSR イニシアチブ委員会"を 2005 年 2 月に設立した．当委員会設立のねらいは，CSR の経営理念や行動憲章，行動基準などを普及させるとともに，日本における CSR の取組みにドライブをかけ，持続可能な社会と企業の発展に寄与することにある．

当委員会の活動の一環として，実際に企業が CSR を進めていく上での羅針盤ともなる"CSR イニシアチブ～経営理念・行動憲章・行動基準～"を書籍の形でこのたび発表するに至った．この"CSR イニシアチブ"は，当委員会が母体である CSR 研究部会における約 1 年間の研究成果をもとに制定したもので，その概要は次のとおりである．

まず，企業が CSR に取り組む上で最も重要となる"CSR 経営理念"を制定

した．次いで，消費者，従業員ほか，合計10のマルチ・ステークホルダーに対して，CSRを進める際の指針となる考え方を，法的責任，経済的責任，倫理的責任，社会貢献的責任の四つの責任レベルから，合計40の"CSR行動憲章"を制定した．

そして，上記CSR行動憲章を具体的な行動基準までブレークダウンして，"CSR行動基準"を制定した．この行動基準は，10のステークホルダーを対象に，四つの責任に基づき実際の企業行動レベルまで詳細に記述し，合計250の"CSR行動基準"で構成されている．

また，グローバル時代といわれる今日，企業は"社会の公器"であると同時に，今後は"世界の公器"ともなる．その意味から我々は今回，日本語版とあわせてビジネスの共通言語である英語に訳し，対訳としてCSRイニシアチブを制定した．

極力，世界中の多くの企業で活用願えるように配慮したつもりではあるが，国家的事情や，取組み企業の財やサービスの形態，また業種や現在の企業環境によって，自社にあわせた加筆・修正が必要かもしれない．その点は考慮願った上で，積極的な活用をお願いしたい．

こうした研究活動が継続できるのも日本経営倫理学会のプロジェクトという産学協同研究の場をいただいたことによるものであり，その意味から水谷雅一学会長をはじめ全役員の方々，さらには学会員の皆様にも心から感謝申し上げなければならない．

また，今回の出版にあたっては，日本規格協会理事の若井博雄氏，並びに，内容及び校正面で適切なアドバイスをいただいた同協会の末安いづみ氏にもお礼申し上げたい．

最後に，このCSRイニシアチブが，日本企業だけでなく，世界中の企業がCSRに取り組む際の一助になれば望外の喜びである．

2005年4月1日

日本経営倫理学会・CSRイニシアチブ委員会
代表　水尾　順一

Member (continued)

"Stakeholder" category that it took charge of writing	Contributor
Mass media	Masafumi Akashi, Corporate officer, General Manager, Corporate Communications Department, Polus Co., Ltd. Yu Tanabe, Researcher, Corporate Social Responsibility Project, Advertising Bureau, Nihon Keizai Shimbun, Inc.
Administration	Keiko Yokoyama, Instructor, Tokai University Nobuki Sato, General Manager, Compliance Group, Audit Department, Mitsui Fudosan Co., Ltd. Toru Yamawaki, Counselor, Kyodo Advertising Co., Ltd.
NPOs/NGOs	Emiko Magoshi, Ph.D., Professor, College of Business and Public Administration, Obirin University Kenkichi Yamaguchi, Chairman, Business Ethics Institute Masahiko Saito, Former Manager, Communications, Novaritis Pharma K.K.
International Community	Hidetaka Oizumi, Personnel Department, East Japan Railway Company Junichi Mizuo, Ph.D., Professor of Business Administration, Surugadai University Masahiko Kon, Executive Officer, Group Finance and Administration & Group Corporate Social Responsibility, Fast Retailing Co., Ltd.

Secretariat of CSR INITIATIVE Committee: Toshio Ariu, Senior Researcher, Socio-economic Research Center, Central Research Institute of Electric Power Industry (CRIEPI)
Address: 1-6-1 Ohtemachi, Chiyoda-ku, Tokyo 100-8126 JAPAN,
Tel.: +81 3-3201-6601, Fax.: +81 3-3287-2864, E-mail: ariu@criepi.denken.or.jp

目　次

推薦のことば ……………………………………………………… 3
まえがき …………………………………………………………… 5
CSR イニシアチブ委員会 ………………………………………… 7

CSR イニシアチブ作成の経緯及び概要

序　文 ……………………………………………………………… 15
1. CSR 経営理念 ………………………………………………… 17
2. CSR 行動憲章 ………………………………………………… 23
3. CSR 行動基準（合計 250 の行動基準）…………………… 29
4. CSR イニシアチブの活用にあたって ……………………… 31

CSR イニシアチブ
〜 CSR 経営理念・行動憲章・行動基準 〜

CSR 経営理念 …………………………………………………… 37
CSR 行動憲章 …………………………………………………… 39
CSR 行動基準 …………………………………………………… 55
　　I.　　消費者 …………………………………………… 55
　　II.　　取引先 …………………………………………… 67
　　III.　　従業員 …………………………………………… 79
　　IV.　　株主・投資家 ……………………………………… 95
　　V.　　地域社会・地球環境 ……………………………… 103
　　VI.　　競争会社 ………………………………………… 113
　　VII.　　マスメディア …………………………………… 121
　　VIII.　行政 ………………………………………………… 129
　　IX.　　NPO/NGO ……………………………………… 135
　　X.　　国際社会 ………………………………………… 143

参考文献・資料 ………………………………………………… 154
賛同組織・団体一覧 …………………………………………… 156

Contents

CSR INITIATIVE Committee ⋯⋯⋯⋯⋯⋯⋯⋯⋯⋯⋯⋯⋯⋯⋯⋯⋯⋯⋯⋯⋯⋯ 8

Background for the development and the general outline of CSR INITIATIVE

Introduction ⋯⋯⋯⋯⋯⋯⋯⋯⋯⋯⋯⋯⋯⋯⋯⋯⋯⋯⋯⋯⋯⋯⋯⋯⋯⋯⋯⋯⋯ 14
1. CSR Management Philosophy ⋯⋯⋯⋯⋯⋯⋯⋯⋯⋯⋯⋯⋯⋯⋯⋯⋯⋯ 16
2. CSR Charter of Conduct ⋯⋯⋯⋯⋯⋯⋯⋯⋯⋯⋯⋯⋯⋯⋯⋯⋯⋯⋯⋯ 22
3. CSR Code of Conduct (250 Codes) ⋯⋯⋯⋯⋯⋯⋯⋯⋯⋯⋯⋯⋯⋯ 28
4. Using the CSR INITIATIVE ⋯⋯⋯⋯⋯⋯⋯⋯⋯⋯⋯⋯⋯⋯⋯⋯⋯⋯ 30

CSR INITIATIVE
~ CSR Management Philosophy, Charter of Conduct and Code of Conduct ~

CSR Management Philosophy ⋯⋯⋯⋯⋯⋯⋯⋯⋯⋯⋯⋯⋯⋯⋯⋯⋯⋯⋯ 36
CSR Charter of Conduct ⋯⋯⋯⋯⋯⋯⋯⋯⋯⋯⋯⋯⋯⋯⋯⋯⋯⋯⋯⋯⋯ 38
CSR Code of Conduct ⋯⋯⋯⋯⋯⋯⋯⋯⋯⋯⋯⋯⋯⋯⋯⋯⋯⋯⋯⋯⋯⋯ 54
    I. Consumers ⋯⋯⋯⋯⋯⋯⋯⋯⋯⋯⋯⋯⋯⋯⋯⋯⋯⋯⋯⋯⋯ 54
    II. Suppliers and Customers ⋯⋯⋯⋯⋯⋯⋯⋯⋯⋯⋯⋯⋯⋯ 66
    III. Employees ⋯⋯⋯⋯⋯⋯⋯⋯⋯⋯⋯⋯⋯⋯⋯⋯⋯⋯⋯⋯⋯ 78
    IV. Shareholders and Investors ⋯⋯⋯⋯⋯⋯⋯⋯⋯⋯⋯⋯⋯ 94
    V. Local Communities and Global Environment ⋯⋯⋯⋯⋯ 102
    VI. Competitors ⋯⋯⋯⋯⋯⋯⋯⋯⋯⋯⋯⋯⋯⋯⋯⋯⋯⋯⋯⋯ 112
    VII. Mass Media ⋯⋯⋯⋯⋯⋯⋯⋯⋯⋯⋯⋯⋯⋯⋯⋯⋯⋯⋯⋯ 120
    VIII. Administration ⋯⋯⋯⋯⋯⋯⋯⋯⋯⋯⋯⋯⋯⋯⋯⋯⋯⋯ 128
    IX. NPOs/NGOs ⋯⋯⋯⋯⋯⋯⋯⋯⋯⋯⋯⋯⋯⋯⋯⋯⋯⋯⋯⋯ 134
    X. International Community ⋯⋯⋯⋯⋯⋯⋯⋯⋯⋯⋯⋯⋯⋯ 142

CSR イニシアチブ 作成の経緯及び概要

Background for the development and the general outline of CSR INITIATIVE

日本文を奇数ページ，英訳を偶数ページに示します．
また，英訳については，必要と思われる部分を要約し，紹介します．

The Japanese version is shown on the right-hand page, the corresponding English on the left.
The English is not identical to the original Japanese, but expresses what the authors deemed necessary to convey.

Background for the development and the general outline of CSR INITIATIVE

Introduction
With continuing advances in the pace of globalization and information technology development, raging competition in the world's markets, and harsh criticisms coming from consumers and communities alike to target corporate practices, interests in the concept of CSR (Corporate Social Responsibilities) are mounting. As ways to draw global attention on fulfilling CSR, the goal of coexistence between business enterprises on one hand and the environment, economy and society on the other assumes an increasingly important tone from a standpoint of sustainable growth of corporations.

The Japan Society for Business Ethics Study, as the most leading academic circle in this field, launched the CSR Research Workshop in May 2004 in an industry-university joint effort to work on its implementation. The CSR Research Workshop has now formed the CSR Initiative Committee since February 2005 with a membership of about 30, including college professors, scholars, businessmen and members of NPOs (Non-Profit Organizations).

CSR イニシアチブ
作成の経緯及び概要

序　文

　近年，グローバリゼーションや情報技術の発展，国際市場における競争激化，消費者をはじめ社会から企業行動への厳しい批判などを背景に，CSR（Corporate Social Responsibility：企業の社会的責任）への関心が高まっている．その取組みが世界的レベルで注目される中で，企業と環境・経済・社会との共生が，企業の持続可能な発展の視点から重要なテーマとなってきた．

　これらを背景に，2004 年 6 月にストックホルムで開催された ISO（International Organization for Standardization：国際標準化機構）の国際会議で，CSR の規格化（SR 規格）が決定した．現在，世界各国で CSR への取組みが進展しており，日本においても経済産業省を中心に進められている．

　日本経営倫理学会では，この領域に最も近い学会として，産学協同の CSR 研究部会を 2004 年 5 月から発足し，精力的に活動を進めてきた．この研究部会は，さかのぼること 2001 年 4 月に発足した SMIX 21（Stakeholder Management Index 21：ステークホルダーマネジメント指標 21）プロジェクト研究メンバーを母体としてスタートしたものである．当プロジェクトの研究成果は，既に研究書籍として 2004 年 5 月に，『CSR マネジメント―ステークホルダーとの共生と企業の社会的責任』（生産性出版）として世に発表している．

　このたび，当研究部会では，大学教授や研究者，企業人，NPO など約 30 名のメンバーで構成される "CSR イニシアチブ委員会" を 2005 年 2 月に設

As part of its activity, the CSR INITIATIVE Committee has established the "CSR INITIATIVE ~ CSR Management Philosophy, Charter of Conduct and Code of Conduct ~" as Figure 1 (p.18) sets forth.

> First, the term "CSR" is defined as a scheme of institutional obligation or responsibility of a corporation to work in-house and outside to make a positive contribution to the advancement of the society while preventing the eruption of corporate scandals to foster and drive the sound development of its own corporate organization and society.

The CSR INITIATIVE is an organized definition of the Management Philosophy, Charter of Conduct and Code of Conduct that should guide corporations in striving towards the fulfillment of CSR.

1. CSR Management Philosophy

Now is the time for corporations to coexist with the society and share enjoyment with it. Neither the growth of a corporation in defiance of the society nor that of the society achieved at the sacrifice of corporations should be

立した．当委員会設立のねらいは，CSR の経営理念や行動憲章，行動基準などを普及させるとともに，日本における CSR の取組みにドライブをかけ，持続可能な社会と企業の発展に寄与することにある．

その活動の一環として，実際に企業が CSR を進めていく上での羅針盤ともなる CSR 経営理念・行動憲章・行動基準を"CSR イニシアチブ"（図1, p.19）として，当委員会で制定した．なお，この CSR イニシアチブは，母体である CSR 研究部会における約1年間の研究成果をもとに検討が加えられて完成したものである．

今後，CSR イニシアチブは，"CSR イニシアチブ委員会"のもとで推進していくこととなる．

最初に，SMIX 21 の研究活動で提起した CSR の考え方を継承し，CSR を次のように定義する．

> CSR とは，企業組織と社会の健全な発展を保護し，促進することを目的として，不祥事の発生を未然に防ぐとともに，社会に積極的に貢献していくために企業の内外に働きかける制度的義務又は責任である．

その上で，CSR 経営理念・行動憲章・行動基準のそれぞれの内容を次のように規定する．

1. CSR 経営理念

企業は社会とともに生き，ともに喜びを享受すべき時代である．社会を無視した企業だけの発展は認められるものではなく，また企業を犠牲にした社会の発展も考えられるものではない．企業と社会は，良好な関係を維持しつつ，相

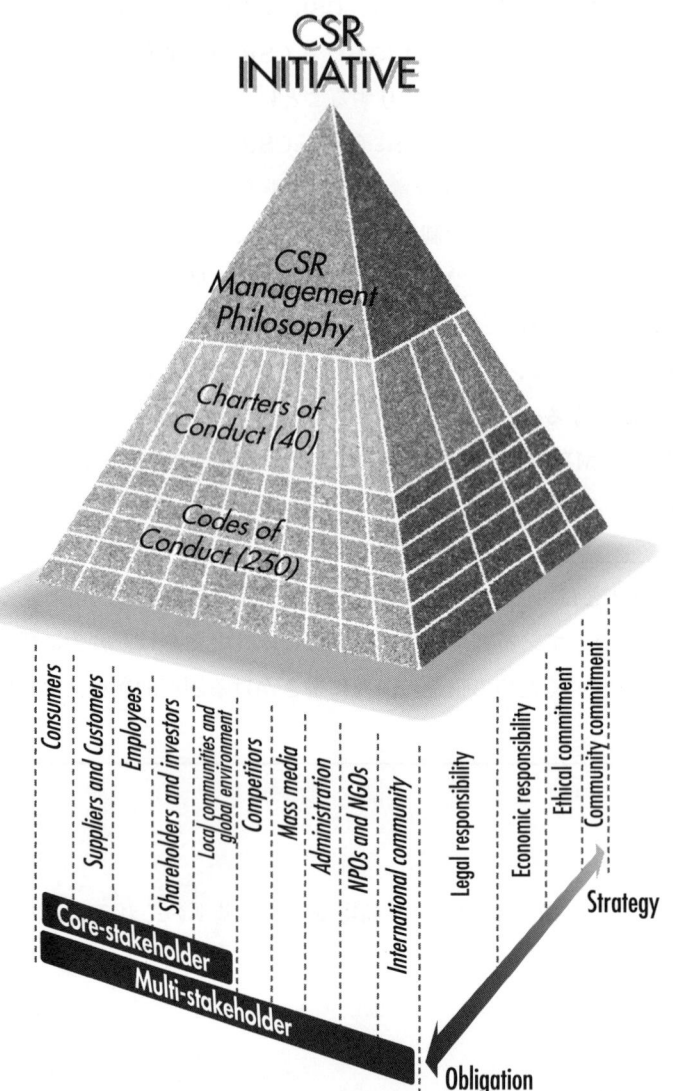

Figure 1 CSR INITIATIVE

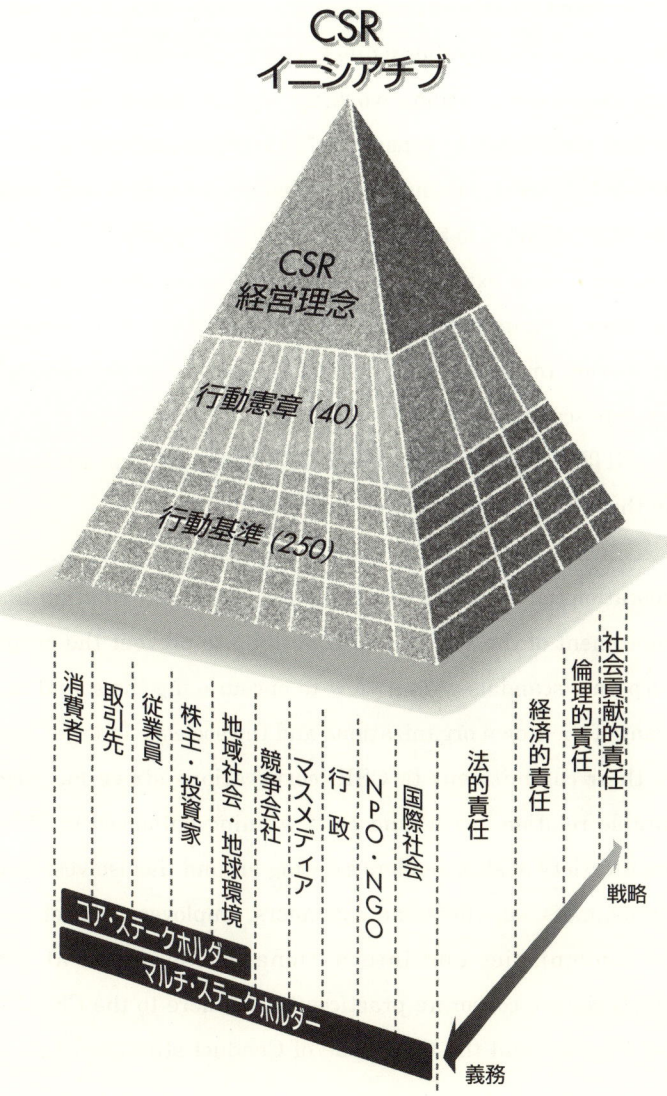

図1　CSRイニシアチブ

taken for granted. Corporations and the society should pursue mutual growth in support of each other while keeping up favorable relations.

This amounts to corporations working with a variety of stakeholders, including but not limited to consumers[*], suppliers and customers, employees, shareholders, local communities, global environments and international communities at large, to build "a co-prosperous society."

Corporations are thus expected to promote the sound growth of the society, as well as their own organizations. To this end, they need to make a positive contribution to the advancement of the society while working to prevent corporate scandals.

The CSR INITIATIVE has formulated a CSR Management Philosophy that builds on these key concepts, which reads as follows:

> Corporations are expected to make a positive contribution to the advancement of the society while working to prevent the eruption of corporate scandals with a view to encouraging the sound development of their own organizations and the society. In order to execute their commitment to CSR, corporations strive for forging favorable relations with, and thus winning enhanced confidence from, a variety of stakeholders existing around themselves, including consumers, suppliers and customers, employees, shareholders, local communities and international communities at large, through sincere corporate practices that adhere to the CSR Charter of Conduct and the CSR Code of Conduct stipulated below, in

---

[*] The term "consumer" as used in the CSR INITIATIVE may be construed to refer to a customer as well if it is a stakeholder directly connected with a corporation in the form of purchasing its products or services. Accordingly, the term "consumer" is used in its broadest sense to cover customers.

互に支えあいながらともに発展を志していかなければならない．

それは企業の多様な利害関係者といわれる消費者＊，取引先，従業員，株主・投資家，地域社会・地球環境，さらには広く国際社会など多様なステークホルダーと企業が，"ともに栄える社会"を構築することを意味している．

したがって，CSRの根本には企業自らの組織に加えて，社会の健全な発展を促進することが求められる．また，そのために，企業は不祥事を未然に防ぐだけでなく，積極的に社会に貢献していくことが必要となる．

これらの基本的なポリシーをもとに，CSRイニシアチブではCSR経営理念を次のとおり作成した．

　企業は，自らの組織と社会の健全な発展を促進することを目的として，不祥事の発生を未然に防ぐとともに，社会に積極的に貢献することが求められている．そのために企業は，次のCSR行動憲章，CSR行動基準をもとに，誠実な企業行動で，消費者，取引先，従業員，株主・投資家，地域社会・地球環境，さらには広く国際社会など，企業を取り巻く多様なステークホルダーとの良好な関係性を構築し信頼感を高めつつ，企業と社会の持続可能な発展を目指す．

＊ CSRイニシアチブでいう"消費者"は，製品やサービスを使用又は消費する直接の消費者だけではない．今後消費者になるかもしれない潜在的な消費者も含む．また，企業によってはお客様，顧客という表現もあることから，それらも含めた広い概念として使用していることに注意されたい．

> pursuit of sustainable development for both themselves and the society.

2. CSR Charter of Conduct

Five kinds of "core stakeholders" chosen to have a close bearing on corporations are: consumers, suppliers and customers, shareholders and investors, local communities, and the global environment.

With the subsequent addition of competitors, mass media, administrations, NPOs/NGOs (Non-Governmental Organizations), and the international community, the population of core stakeholders above has been expanded to identify a total of 10 multi-stakeholders.

Guiding principles in driving CSR with these 10 multi-stakeholders have then been classified into the following levels of responsibility to work out a total of 40 CSR Charters of Conduct:

(1) Legal Responsibility

As the wording "Law is the minimum limit of ethics" suggests, the legal responsibility is a minimum of responsibility that corporations accredited as social entities are obliged to fulfill. The importance of legal responsibility should be self-explanatory as many corporations ban corporate practices in violation of laws and regulations.

After all, legal responsibilities are to ensure the safety of citizens' lives and to prevent legal violations and unfair trade in the course of corporate activity. Legal responsibility is a necessary condition for a corporation to be accredited as a social entity but is not a sufficient condition. It should be viewed as a minimum of responsibility in terms of the significance of corporate existence.

2. CSR 行動憲章

　CSR 経営理念の実現にあたって，働きかける対象としての消費者，取引先，従業員，株主・投資家，地域社会・地球環境の五つは，企業との関係が特に深い"核となるステークホルダー"（コア・ステークホルダー）とした．

　コア・ステークホルダーに加えて，競争会社，マスメディア，行政，NPO（Non-Profit Organization：民間非営利組織）/NGO（Non-Governmental Organization：非政府組織），国際社会を含めた合計 10 のマルチ・ステークホルダーを特定し，これらのマルチ・ステークホルダーに対して，CSR を進める際の指針となる考え方を次のとおり四つの責任レベルに区分し，CSR 行動憲章として制定した．

(1) 法的責任

　第 1 は"法的責任"である．"法は倫理の最下限"という言葉が示しているとおり，社会的存在として認められた企業が果たすべき最低限度の責任である．多くの企業が法令に違反した企業行動をとることを禁止していることからも，その重要性は理解される．

　例えば，消費者には安心・安全，地域社会に対しては環境対応など法律や条例を中心とした社会のルールを尊重してこそ，その存在意義がある．また，従業員に対してはサービス残業の禁止，男女共同参画法の遵守など現在の日本企業が抱える領域もここにはある．さらに取引先に対しては，下請法（略称）の遵守や独占禁止法による公正な取引の遵守などがある．

　つまり，市民の生命の安全を保護し，企業行動においては法律違反や不公正な取引の発生を未然に予防する責任である．ただし，企業が社会的存在として認められる必要条件ではあるが，それでよしとする十分条件ではない．あくまでも企業の存在意義を考える意味で，最低限度の責任として法的責任はとらえ

(2) Economic Responsibility

Once a corporation's legal responsibility is fulfilled, the next step is to fulfill its economic responsibility for its stakeholders, or that of paying results to its shareholders as dividends, paying wages and remunerations to its employees in consideration for their labor, paying taxes to the nation and local communities, and paying due prices to its suppliers.

Some view economic responsibility as the primary responsibility, but we advocate legal responsibility as such. Considering the fact that corporate scandals in various countries the world over have undermined the existence of businesses, legal responsibility should be deserved prime emphasis.

(3) Ethical Commitment

Ethical commitment is that imposed by voluntary standards or restraints in the industry or by a company-specific sense of ethics beyond the boundaries of legal regulations. Ethical commitment can be thought of three broad parts: human rights and the labor environment, consumer relation, and global environment protection.

While legal responsibility sets a minimum of responsibility to be fulfilled in connection with corporate activity, ethic commitment is positioned as a challenging task set by the industry or a corporation on its own and serves as a key element in the formulation of corporate strategies.

られるべきである．

(2) 経済的責任

　法的責任が遂行された段階では，企業は第2の責任として"経済的責任"を果たさなければならない．株主に対しては成果配分としての配当であり，従業員に対しては労働の対価としての賃金・報酬であり，国家・地域社会に対しては税金である．また，取引先に対しては支払うべき正当な価格など，企業を取り巻くステークホルダーに対する経済的責任を指す．

　ただし，ここで注意しなければならないのは，経済的責任は法的責任と重なる部分も存在することであり，例えば，最低賃金は労働基準法で規定されていることから，経済的責任でいう賃金は法的責任を越えたレベルであるということができる．

　米国の経営学者のアーチ・キャロルのように，経済的責任を第一義的責任とする考え方もあるが，我々は法的責任を第一義として提起している．日本は法治国家であり，そこにおいて企業が存在できるのは，法令遵守という最低限の責任を果たすことでその存在意義が認められると考える．また，現在の世界各国での企業不祥事で，企業の存続さえも失う現実を考えた場合，法的責任を最優先させるべき意味からも第一の責任とみるべきである．

(3) 倫理的責任

　第3は"倫理的責任"を掲げた．法律の規制を越えたところでの業界や企業独自の倫理観に基づく自主基準や自主規制による責任としての"倫理的責任"である．倫理的責任は，次のとおり大別して三つの領域から考えることができる．

　① 人権・労働環境の領域

　この領域には，劣悪な環境での労働や過酷な労働などへの自主規制がある．また，年齢や性別，国籍，身体の障害の有無といった区別を越え，多様性を尊重した採用や役員への登用等もこれに該当する．例えば，育児・介護の支援や従業員の多様な働き方への支援活動，さらには女性管理職比率の向上など女性の活性化にかかわる男女共同参画推進企業としての課題などもここにはある．

(4) Community Commitment

The last concept, community commitment covers a package of positive activities, including the protection of consumer benefits, approaches to social contribution and cultural aid projects, global environment protection, and more active commitments in relevant areas.

It includes in-house programs designed to back up active contributions to local communities, such as granting paid leaves to volunteering employees and otherwise valuing employees. All these efforts should be approached as socially desirable activities from a strategic perspective.

Corporations should approach these four areas of responsibility as a minimum of obligations they ought to fulfill. Economic responsibility to pay wages to employees and taxes to the nation is also a legitimate obligation for a corporation as a social entity.

② 消費者対応の領域

製品の返品や交換の自由を保証する"顧客満足保証"活動，その他，消費者に対する安全・安心対応に向けた相談やクレーム対応を行うお客様相談センターなどの活動もこの領域である．

③ 地球環境保護の領域

例えば，環境マネジメントシステムの導入，工場における自然エネルギーの採用や二酸化炭素排出の自主規制，廃棄物のリサイクルや化学物質の使用制限，水質汚濁に関する法律以上の自主目標の設定などがある．それ以外にも，環境会計やLCA (Life Cycle Assessment：ライフサイクルアセスメント) の導入，グリーン購入の推進，廃棄物の削減，環境・サステナビリティ報告書や展示会を利用した環境コミュニケーションなどがある．

第1の法的責任が企業行動に関連して最低限度守るべき下限線であるのに対して，この倫理的責任は業界や企業が独自に設定した努力目標として位置付けられ，今後重要な企業戦略上の要素となる．

(4) 社会貢献的責任

第4は，消費者利益の保護，社会貢献・文化支援活動への取組み，そして，地球環境保護，さらには積極的な貢献活動への取組みなど，ポジティブな活動も含んだ"社会貢献的責任"の考え方である．

社内に対しては，ボランティア休暇制度による支援や，地域社会に対する積極的貢献活動への支援など，社会貢献活動をバックアップする体制や，従業員を重視するプログラムであり，社会的に望ましい活動として戦略的発想で取り組む必要がある．

そして，この四つの責任について企業が取り組むスタンスは，法的責任は企業が最低限に守るべき"義務"であり，また経済的責任の従業員への給料支払いや地域・国家への税金の支払いもまた社会的存在として果たすべき当然の義務である．倫理的責任や社会貢献的責任は，人，物，金などの限られた経営資

Ethical commitment and community commitment may be thought of as task of management strategy from a standpoint of identifying in which area one should invest limited managerial resources, such as manpower, materials and money, and how much. The higher a level of responsibility is, the closer it gets to corporate company-wide strategic significance. Figure 2 depicts these four areas of responsibility.

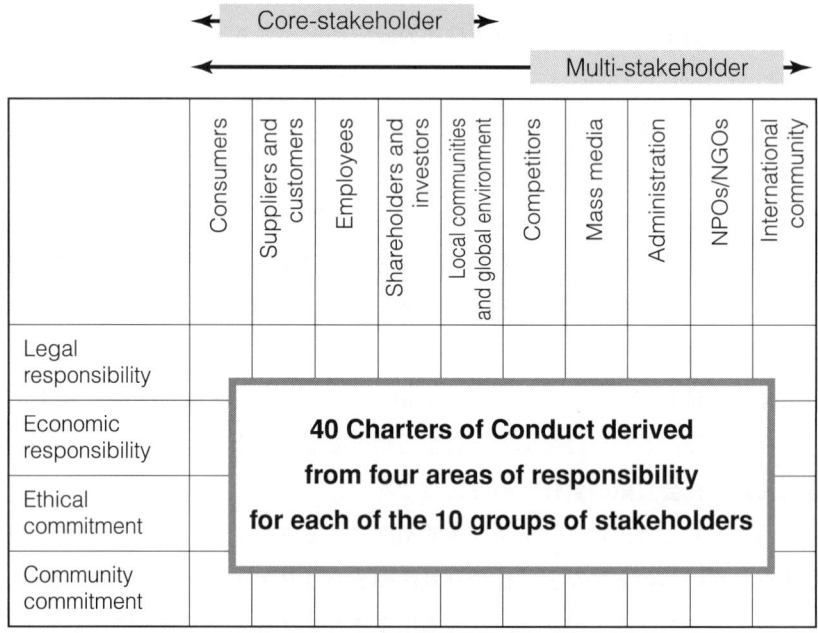

Figure 2 CSR Charters of Conduct

3. CSR Code of Conduct (250 Codes)

The CSR Charter of Conduct is broken down into CSR Code of Conduct at the working level of corporate activity

The Charter is particularized at the working level of corporate activity on the basis of four areas of responsibility for each of the 10 groups of stake-

源をどの領域にどれだけ投資するかという視点を考えれば経営戦略的レベルということができ，上位の責任レベルほど企業の全社戦略的要素が強くなる．

これらの四つの責任を，図2に示す．

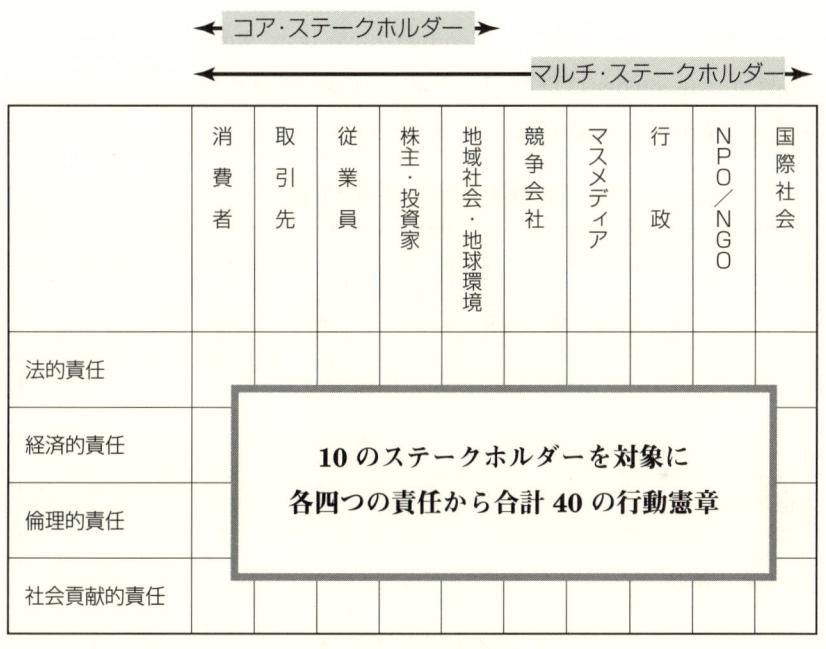

図2　CSR行動憲章

3. CSR行動基準（合計250の行動基準）

CSR行動憲章を具体的な行動基準にまでブレークダウンしたものが，CSR行動基準である．

10のステークホルダーを対象に，四つの責任に基づき実際の企業行動レベルまで詳細に記述することによって，経営トップから従業員まで価値観が共有

holders, so the whole company, from the leaders down to the employees, can share their values.

A total of 250 CSR Codes of Conduct have been worked out for the 10 groups of stakeholders (Table 1). For more detailed definitions of the CSR Charter of Conduct and CSR Code of Conduct, see the text.

Table 1 CSR Code of Conduct

	Consumers	Suppliers and customers	Employees	Shareholders and investors	Local communities and global environment	Competitors	Mass media	Administration	NPOs/NGOs	International community	Total
Legal responsibility	14	13	14	6	8	8	4	4	5	9	85
Economic responsibility	3	4	8	6	3	2	5	2	4	10	47
Ethical commitment	10	12	12	5	5	6	4	5	5	8	72
Community commitment	3	3	8	4	7	6	3	3	4	5	46
Total	30	32	42	21	23	22	16	14	18	32	250

4. Using the CSR INITIATIVE

In the present era of globalization, corporations are public institutions of

化できる．すなわち，行動憲章が行動基準で明確にされることで，いわゆる暗黙知が形式知に変換されることとなる．

制定にあたっては，日本経済団体連合会の企業行動憲章や ILO（International Labor Organization：国際労働機関）の宣言，人権と労働に関する規格 SA（Social Accontability：社会説明責任）8000，コー円卓会議の企業行動指針，さらには松下電器産業，資生堂他グローバル企業の行動基準など，既にある基準や指針等も踏まえて制定している．

ここでは 10 のステークホルダーを対象に，合計 250 の CSR 行動基準を制定した（表 1）．CSR 行動憲章と行動基準の詳細は本文を参照願いたい．

表1 CSR 行動基準

	消費者	取引先	従業員	株主・投資家	地域社会・地球環境	競争会社	マスメディア	行政	NPO/NGO	国際社会	合計
法的責任	14	13	14	6	8	8	4	4	5	9	85
経済的責任	3	4	8	6	3	2	5	2	4	10	47
倫理的責任	10	12	12	5	5	6	4	5	5	8	72
社会貢献的責任	3	3	8	4	7	6	3	3	4	5	46
合計	30	32	42	21	23	22	16	14	18	32	250

4. CSR イニシアチブの活用にあたって

グローバル時代といわれる今日，企業は"社会の公器"であると同時に，今

the society and, possibly in the future, of the world. Corporations should share their values with their stakeholders the world over, including its employees, customer and suppliers.

In the present-day world of ubiquitous computing, news about bad as well as good corporate practices momentarily travel worldwide as corporate information. By having the CSR INITIATIVE publicized to the world's consumers and local communities or sharing its value with them, corporations would be able to fulfill their responsibility of its corporate transparency and accountability.

The CSR INITIATIVE is now available in English as well as Japanese versions. The CSR INITIATIVE is intended by itself to fit into as many corporations in the world as possible, but it is open to customization to meet specific national conditions, the forms of goods and services dealt in by working corporations, their industries and corporate climates and other corporation-specific needs before it can be put to extensive use.

Lastly, it is the publisher's hope that this CSR INITIATIVE will aid global enterprises in their approach to fulfilling their own CSR.

後は"世界の公器"ともなる．企業は，全世界の自社の利害関係者である従業員や取引先，供給業者などとその価値観を共有しなければならない．

一方，現在のユビキタス社会では，インターネットなどを通じて，善行も悪事も瞬時のうちに企業情報として世界に伝播する．全世界の消費者や地域社会などすべてのステークホルダーに CSR イニシアチブを開示し，又は逆にその価値観を共有化することで，企業の透明性や説明責任も果たせることとなる．

その意味から我々は今回，日本語版とあわせて共通言語の英語で対訳して，CSR イニシアチブを制定した．極力多くの企業で活用願えるように配慮したつもりではあるが，取組み企業の財やサービスの形態，また業種や現在の企業環境によって，自社にあわせた加筆・修正が必要かもしれない．

また，中小企業であれば，ステークホルダーとして消費者，取引先，従業員の三つ，責任レベルとして法的責任，経済的責任，倫理的責任の三つに限定した活用でもよい．そして，毎年新たな行動基準の目標を設定したり，段階的に検討すべき行動基準を拡大したりすることも可能である．

すなわち，ここで取り上げた 10 のステークホルダー，四つの責任に該当する行動基準すべてを最初から網羅的に検討すべきというわけではない．まず企業ごとに対象とするステークホルダー，責任のレベルを明確にし，その上で行動基準に対する評価を行うことが得策である．これらの点を考慮願った上で，積極的な活用をお願いしたい．

CSR イニシアチブ
~ CSR 経営理念・行動憲章・行動基準 ~

CSR INITIATIVE
~ CSR Management Philosophy, Charter of Conduct and Code of Conduct ~

日本経営倫理学会
CSR イニシアチブ委員会

CSR INITIATIVE Committee
Japan Society for Business Ethics Study

日本文を奇数ページ，英訳を偶数ページに示します．

The Japanese version is shown on the right-hand page, the corresponding English on the left.

CSR INITIATIVE

~ CSR Management Philosophy, Charter of Conduct and Code of Conduct ~

CSR INITIATIVE Committee
Japan Society for Business Ethics Study

CSR Management Philosophy

Corporations are expected to make a positive contribution to the advancement of the society while working to prevent the eruption of corporate scandals with a view to encouraging the sound development of their own organizations and the society. In order to execute their commitment to Corporate Social Responsibilities, corporations strive for forging favorable relations with, and thus winning enhanced confidence from, a variety of stakeholders existing around themselves, including consumers, suppliers & customers, employees, shareholders & investors, local communities and international communities at large, through sincere corporate practices that adhere to the CSR Charter of Conduct and the CSR Code of Conduct stipulated below, in pursuit of sustainable development for both themselves and the society.

CSR イニシアチブ
～CSR 経営理念・行動憲章・行動基準～

日本経営倫理学会
CSR イニシアチブ委員会

CSR 経営理念

　企業は，自らの組織と社会の健全な発展を促進することを目的として，不祥事の発生を未然に防ぐとともに，社会に積極的に貢献することが求められている．そのために企業は，次の CSR 行動憲章，CSR 行動基準をもとに，誠実な企業行動で，消費者，取引先，従業員，株主・投資家，地域社会，さらには広く国際社会など，企業を取り巻く多様なステークホルダーとの良好な関係性を構築し信頼感を高めつつ，企業と社会の持続可能な発展を目指す．

CSR Charter of Conduct

I. Consumers

1. **Legal Responsibility**

   To act with prime emphasis on complying with all the laws and regulations relevant to consumers to protect their safety and security.

2. **Economic Responsibility**

   To pursue proper functionality and fair pricing for the products and services provided by corporations from consumer-oriented perspectives to offer economic values to customers.

3. **Ethical Commitment**

   To place consumer benefits above anything in all aspects of corporate activity, as by preventing and dissolving consumer complaints and encouraging a consumer participation-oriented way of management to better reflect consumer views, thereby pursuing greater customer satisfaction actively through sincere corporate practices.

4. **Community Commitment**

   To make an active contribution to customers to win their confidence and sympathy, thereby relieving and assisting the socially vulnerable as a whole and building a barrier-free community.

II. Suppliers & Customers

1. **Legal Responsibility**

   To comply with all applicable legal requirements in dealing with all suppliers and customers and respect the fulfillment of contracts pursuant to proper market rules and fair corporate activities to promote equal and fair trade relations with them.

CSR 行動憲章

I. 消費者
1. 法的責任
消費者にかかわるあらゆる法令を遵守し，消費者の安全・安心を守ることを第一として行動する．

2. 経済的責任
企業が提供する製品やサービスに関して，消費者重視の視点から適正機能と適正価格を追求し，消費者に経済的な価値を提供する．

3. 倫理的責任
消費者の不平・不満を予防・解消し，意見を反映させた消費者参加指向の経営を促進するなど，すべての企業活動に消費者利益を最優先とし，誠実な企業行動で消費者満足を積極的に追求する．

4. 社会貢献的責任
社会的弱者全般に対する救済・支援，さらにはバリアフリー社会の構築を目的として，消費者に対して積極的に貢献することで消費者から信頼と共感を得る．

II. 取引先
1. 法的責任
すべての取引先との関係において，関連法令を遵守し，公正な市場ルールと適正な商慣習に従い，契約を尊重し，対等・公平な取引関係を推進する．

2. **Economic Responsibility**

   To take every conceivable measure to boost the level of technology, develop human resources, manage information and so forth so as to deliver quality products and services that should deserve favorable customer evaluation by working in collaboration with suppliers and customers.

3. **Ethical Commitment**

   To maintain fair and sincere dealings with suppliers and customers on equal partnerships with mutual trust to respect their independent management, pursuing mutual sustainable growth and business prosperity to mutual benefit.

4. **Community Commitment**

   To take active part in making social contributions, conducting conservative activities of global environment and so forth by taking advantage of the characteristics of all supply chain parties so as to stay ready to address urges from the diversity of stakeholders, thereby pursuing mutual co-existence and co-prosperity.

III. Employees

1. **Legal Responsibility**

   To manifest the codes of conduct and house regulations for employees to observe from a primary standpoint of their safety and health to ensure that they fully comply with the applicable laws and regulations.

2. **Economic Responsibility**

   To ensure that employees can maximize their abilities on the basis of their own individuality and ingenuity and that corporations are committed to fair employment practice at the stage of hiring, giving

2. **経済的責任**

   企業と取引先が相互に協力して,消費者に評価される良質な製品やサービスを提供できるよう,技術水準の向上,人材の育成,情報管理等に万全の配慮を行う.

3. **倫理的責任**

   企業と取引先が相互の信頼に基づき,対等なパートナーとして自主的経営を尊重し,相互の持続可能な発展と事業の繁栄を目指して,公正で誠実な取引を行う.

4. **社会貢献的責任**

   多様なステークホルダーの要請にこたえられるように,企業と取引先が相互に本業の特性を生かしながら,社会貢献,地球環境保全活動などに積極的に取り組み,共存共栄を図る.

III. 従業員

1. **法的責任**

   企業は,従業員の安全と健康を第一に考え,守るべき行動基準や社内規則を明示し,法令遵守を徹底する.

2. **経済的責任**

   従業員一人ひとりの個性や創造性に基づく能力を最大限に発揮できるようにするとともに,雇用,機会,評価,処遇等を公正に行う.

opportunities, placing assessment, compensating and other condition of employment.

3. **Ethical Commitment**

   To promote employees' sincere behavior while respecting their diversity, human rights and privacy, thereby expediting the flow of communication between them and the society.

4. **Community Commitment**

   To help each and every employee take active part in the communities as a good member of the corporate citizen.

IV. Shareholders and Investors

1. **Legal Responsibility**

   To carry out appropriate accounting and closing procedures and comply with Generally Accepted Accounting Principle (GAAP), other accounting standards, relevant laws and regulations, such as those that ban insider trading.

2. **Economic Responsibility**

   To actively conduct IR activities targeting shareholders and investors in respect of the continual growth of businesses and the proper dividend practice.

3. **Ethical Commitment**

   To disclose corporate information for shareholders and investors from time to time and in an appropriate manner to promote dialogs with them, thereby improving the transparency of management and enhancing corporate governance.

4. **Community Commitment**

   To position the work of making social contributions and conducting conservative activities of global environment as long-term corporate

3. **倫理的責任**
   従業員の多様性・人権・プライバシーを尊重するとともに誠実な行動を推進し，従業員と社会のコミュニケーションの円滑化に努める．

4. **社会貢献的責任**
   従業員一人ひとりが良き企業市民の一員として，社会に対して積極的にかかわっていくことを支援する．

IV. 株主・投資家

1. **法的責任**
   適正な会計・決算処理を行うとともに，インサイダー取引の禁止など関係する法令・基準を遵守する．

2. **経済的責任**
   株主・投資家に対し，継続的な事業の発展や経営戦略に関するIR活動を積極的に行い，利益の公平・公正な配分を目指す．

3. **倫理的責任**
   株主・投資家に対し，適時・適切に企業情報を公開して対話を促進し，経営の透明性を高め，コーポレートガバナンスを向上させる．

4. **社会貢献的責任**
   社会貢献，地球環境保全活動を企業の長期的な戦略投資として位置付け，社会的評価を高め，ブランド価値の維持・向上を図る．

investment of strategic significance to help acquire augmented social evaluations, thereby sustaining and enhancing the corporate brand value.

V. Local Communities and Global Environment

1. **Legal Responsibility**

    To comply with the laws and regulations, local ordinances, voluntary covenants and other rules that pertain to the environmental conservation, health and safety, security and other relevant aspects of the local communities.

2. **Economic Responsibility**

    To contribute to the development of the local economies through taxation, procurement, employment and so forth.

3. **Ethical Commitment**

    To open dialogs with, and fulfill accountability for, the local communities and respect their histories and cultures, pursuing mutual sound growth and better public welfare; and to promote activities to resolve global environmental problems such as for resource cycling.

4. **Community Commitment**

    To commit an active policy of pursuing coexistence with the local communities as a good global citizen and corporate citizen, by developing and investing in businesses that could lead to the sustainable growth of the local communities and global environment, by providing the corporate managerial resources to promote community support activities.

V. 地域社会・地球環境

1. **法的責任**
   地域社会の環境保全，健康・安全，治安などに関係する法令，地域の条例，自主的な協定等を遵守する．

2. **経済的責任**
   納税や調達，雇用の確保等を通じて，地域経済の発展に寄与する．

3. **倫理的責任**
   地域社会との対話や説明責任を果たし，地域社会の歴史や文化を尊重し，ともに健全な発展や公共の福祉増進等を目指すとともに，地球環境問題の解決に向け，資源の循環等に積極的に取り組む．

4. **社会貢献的責任**
   良き地球市民かつ企業市民として，地域社会や地球環境の持続可能な発展につながる事業の開発・投資や経営資源を生かしたコミュニティ支援活動の推進など，地域社会との共生活動を積極的に進める．

VI. Competitors

1. Legal Responsibility

To comply with all applicable legal requirements in effect at home and abroad without forming cartels or rigging with competitors in violations of the Antitrust Law.

2. Economic Responsibility

To eliminate non-ethical or excessive competition among competitors to pursue fair, transparent and reasonable trade practices.

3. Ethical Commitment

To form favorable partnerships with competitors to win trust from the stakeholders in the market we work.

4. Community Commitment

To promote social contributions, conservative activities of global environment and so forth with competitors as members of the community.

VII. Mass Media

1. Legal Responsibility

To comply with the applicable laws and regulations pertaining to mass media, without releasing falsified statements, infringing on privacy and intellectual property rights and so forth.

2. Economic Responsibility

To disclose factual information of social significance, including financial and accounting information, to mass media from time to time and in an appropriate manner and try to collect opinions directly from the world via the mass media.

3. Ethical Commitment

To disclose information of serious social concern, such as that about defective products or accidents, and negative information, such as

VI. 競争会社

1. 法的責任

競争会社との間で，独占禁止法違反のカルテルや談合を行わず，その他の国内外の法令を遵守する．

2. 経済的責任

競争会社間では，非倫理的又は過度な競争を排除し，公正，透明，適正な取引を行う．

3. 倫理的責任

競争会社との関係では，市場に参加するステークホルダーの信頼を獲得するために，良好なパートナーシップを築く．

4. 社会貢献的責任

競争会社とは，ともに社会の一員として，社会貢献，地球環境保全活動などを推進する．

VII. マスメディア

1. 法的責任

マスメディアに対しては，虚偽発言，プライバシーの侵害，知的財産権の侵害などを行わず，法令を遵守する．

2. 経済的責任

マスメディアに対しては，財務・会計情報を含む社会的に重要な事実情報を適時適切に公開するとともにマスメディアを介した社会の意見などの生の声の収集に努める．

3. 倫理的責任

欠陥製品や事故など，社会生活に重大な影響を与える情報や不祥事等のマイナス情報を遅滞なく開示する．さらにホームページやウェブ等を通じた

that about scandals, to the mass media without delay, and also take advantage of the power of two-way communication via the home page, web and other media.

4. **Community Commitment**

   To disclose corporate information about social contributions, conservative activities of global environment and so forth to the mass media to contribute to the development of the communities as a good corporate citizen.

VIII. Administration

1. **Legal Responsibility**

   To comply with the laws and regulations, local ordinances and other rules that pertain to the creation of a safe and comfortable social environment, the respect of human rights, the sound development of the economy and society, the promotion of public welfare and so forth.

2. **Economic Responsibility**

   To fulfill tax liabilities to the national and local governments by developing sound corporate activities, such as investment, employment and procurement, and yielding profits through appropriate internal control practices.

3. **Ethical Commitment**

   To disclose corporate information positively and take part in the formulation processes of the administrative policy, planning and standards to represent public opinions.

4. **Community Commitment**

   To commit an active policy of developing and investing in businesses that could lead to the sustainable growth of the communities, including the governments, and providing the corporate managerial

双方向のコミュニケーションを活用する．

4. 社会貢献的責任

社会貢献，地球環境保全活動などに関する企業情報をマスメディアに開示することで，良き企業市民としてともに社会の発展に寄与する．

VIII. 行政

1. 法的責任

安全で快適な社会環境の確保，人権尊重，経済・社会の健全な発展，公共の福祉増進などに関係する法令，地域の条例等を遵守する．

2. 経済的責任

投資・雇用・調達を含む健全な企業活動を展開し，適切な社内管理を行って利益を計上し，国と地方の行政に対して納税責任を果たす．

3. 倫理的責任

企業情報を積極的に開示するとともに，行政政策・計画や基準策定に対し，民意の反映を目指し参画する．

4. 社会貢献的責任

良き企業市民として，社会の持続可能な発展につながる事業の開発・投資や，経営資源を生かした行政を含めた社会との共生活動を積極的に進める．

resources to coexist with them as a good corporate citizen.

IX. NPOs/NGOs
1. Legal Responsibility
To comply with all relevant laws and regulations in conducting corporate activities that link or collaborate with organizations involved in non-profit activities, such as NPOs and NGOs.
2. Economic Responsibility
To endeavor to provide donations, technologies, information, human resources and so forth to aid in the work of NPOs and NGOs contributing to the development of the society.
3. Ethical Commitment
To hold active dialogs with NPOs and NGOs and build relationships of collaboration with them on the basis of corporate philosophy and visions.
4. Community Commitment
To take active part in making social contributions, conducting conservative activities of global environment and so forth in collaboration with NPOs and NGOs, by providing the corporate managerial resources.

X. International Community
1. Legal Responsibility
To comply with international rules and guidelines and the laws and regulations pertaining to Japan and the countries of operation as a member of the global society.
2. Economic Responsibility
To contribute to the economic growth of the regions of operation

IX. NPO/NGO
1. 法的責任
NPO/NGO など非営利活動を進める組織との連携，協働等に関係する企業活動においてあらゆる法令を遵守する．

2. 経済的責任
社会の発展に寄与する NPO/NGO などの活動に必要とされる寄付や技術，情報，人材等の提供に努める．

3. 倫理的責任
企業の方針・ビジョンに基づいて，NPO/NGO と積極的に対話し，互いに協働関係を構築する．

4. 社会貢献的責任
企業のもつ経営資源の活用を通じて，NPO/NGO とともに社会貢献，地球環境保全活動などに積極的に参画し，健全な社会の発展に寄与する．

X. 国際社会
1. 法的責任
国際社会の一員として，国際的なルールやガイドライン，日本国及び事業を行う国に関する法令等を遵守する．

2. 経済的責任
事業を行う国の取引慣行を尊重し，公正かつ公平な企業活動を行い，事業

through fair corporate activities in respect of the trade practices in those countries.

3. **Ethical Commitment**

    To contribute to the sustainable development of the countries of operation by holding sincere dialogs with the targeted regions in respect of the cultures, histories and customs in these countries.

4. **Community Commitment**

    To endeavor to conserve and improve limited global resources by working to contribute to the social development of the countries of operation and protecting their natural environments.

を行う地域の経済発展に寄与する．

3. **倫理的責任**

   事業を行う国の文化・歴史・慣習を尊重し，事業を行う地域との対話を誠実に行い，持続可能な発展に寄与する．

4. **社会貢献的責任**

   事業を行う国の発展に資する社会貢献活動を行うとともに，事業を行う地域の自然環境を保護し，限りある地球資源の保全や改善に努める．

CSR Code of Conduct

I. Consumers

1. Legal responsibility

1.1 Safety and Security Assurance

To act on the guiding principle of placing consumer safety and security above anything in all aspects of corporate activity, including the planning of products and services, their research and development, material procurement, manufacturing, logistics, sale and usage by consumers.

1.2 Disclosure of Defects and Troubles

To promptly disclose to consumers any defects or trouble in products or services that could affect consumer safety and security to consumers as they are known and take appropriate action in the circumstances.

1.3 Recall Activities

To publicize detailed information of the products to be recalled both in and outside the company and recover them promptly.

1.4 Fulfilling Accountability

To deliver products or services with accompanying statements of the usage directions, tips on how to prevent misuse and abuse, possible hazards and other relevant information to correctly convey to the customers.

1.5 Proper Labeling and Representation

To act on the principles of proper labeling and representation without improperly labeling products and services, as by false superiority or

CSR 行動基準

I. 消費者

1. 法的責任

1.1 安全・安心の確保

製品やサービスの企画,研究,開発,原料調達,製造,物流,販売そして消費者の使用場面も含めて,すべての企業活動に消費者の安全・安心を最優先すべき基本理念として行動する.

1.2 欠陥・不具合の告知

製品やサービスにおける,消費者の安全・安心に影響する欠陥や不具合が判明した場合は,事実を速やかに消費者に告知し,適切な対応をとる.

1.3 リコール活動

リコール対象製品は社内外に公表するとともに,製品回収は迅速に実施する.

1.4 説明責任の遂行

製品やサービスに関する使用法,誤用・濫用予防,予測される危険性などの説明を文書化して添付し,消費者に正しく伝達する.

1.5 適正な表示・表現

製品やサービスに関する優良・有利誤認,二重価格,誇大表示・表現,虚偽やおとりの表示・表現,原産地の偽装表示などの不当表示を行わず,適正表

advantage recognition, dual pricing, fraudulent labeling and representation, falsified or bait labeling or representation, and falsified origin labeling.

1.6 Proper Premium Campaigning

To conduct premium campaigns in accordance with the Antitrust Law on the basis of the classifications of packaged sale, prize-offered sale and open prizes.

1.7 Ban on Tie-in Sale

To refrain from the tie-in sale of popular items or services with other products.

1.8 Ban on Forcing Resale Price Practice

To refrain from conducting any act of binding on others to maintain legally unjustifiable resale prices or from any conduct suggestive of such act.

1.9 Dumping and Switch Sale

To refrain from dumping products at legally unjustifiable low prices, as by selling them for prices significantly lower than their product costs, and from switch sale that sells products or services for significantly low prices for the purpose of pulling customers to lead to the sale of other, more profit-making products.

1.10 Ban on Forming Cartels

To refrain from making prior arrangements or holding prior negotiations with competitors on the selling or buying prices, production volume, selling quantities, suppliers and customers, sales territories, quality, governing standards, timing and other aspects of products and services in violation of the principles of anti-cartelization.

1.11 Respect of Intellectual Property Rights

To refrain from conducting any act of infringing on intellectual prop-

示・表現に則して行動する．

1.6 適正な景品付きキャンペーン
景品付きキャンペーンは，総付き販売，懸賞付き販売，オープン懸賞の区分をもとに独占禁止法に則して実施する．

1.7 抱き合わせ販売の禁止
人気製品やサービスの販売を条件にした他の製品との抱き合わせ販売は，これを行わない．

1.8 再販売価格維持行為の禁止
法律で認められない再販売価格の維持・拘束行為，またそのことを示唆する言動や行為も行わない．

1.9 不当廉売・おとり販売の禁止
製造原価を著しく下回る価格で継続して販売するなど，法律で認められない不当な価格での廉売や，集客を目的として製品やサービスを著しく低い価格で販売して他の利益製品の販売に結びつける"おとり販売"行為は行わない．

1.10 カルテルの禁止
カルテルとして禁止されている，競争会社間での製品やサービスに関する販売価格や購入価格，生産数量，販売数量，取引先や販売地域，品質，規格，時期などについての取決めや話合いは，これを行わない．

1.11 知的財産権の尊重
特許権や商標権，著作権，実用新案権，意匠権などの知的財産権を侵害する

erty rights, such as patents, trademark rights, copyrights, utility model rights, and design rights, or from conducting any similar conduct that could lead consumers to false recognition or misunderstanding.

1.12 Environmental Conservation Activities

To comply with the laws and regulations pertaining to the goal of environmental conservation, such as those concerning product reduction, recycling and reuse, in all aspects of corporate activity, such as product planning, R&D, manufacture, logistics and consumer usage.

1.13 Protection of Personal Information

To place and safeguard under strict management such personal information that is collected in the course of dealing with consumers to prevent its leakage and illegal, unauthorized and inappropriate use.

1.14 Others

In addition to the items mentioned so far, applicable laws and regulations vary from one type or segment of industry to another, including the Door-to-Door Sales and Other Direct Sales Law and the Installment Sales Law. The scope of CSR code of conduct discussed here is limited to those general laws and regulations that pertain to consumers more closely, leaving aside industry-specific laws. Naturally, the fulfillment of specific corporate or organizational activities may require compliance with these additional laws and with various industry-defined voluntary codes.

2. Economic Responsibility

2.1 Fair Functionality

To provide consumers with economic values by offering products and services with functionality compatible with their pricing from a stand-

行為，また，これらに類似し消費者に誤認や誤解を与える行為や言動は行わない．

1.12　環境保護活動
製品やサービスの企画，研究，開発，製造，物流，そして消費者の使用場面も含むすべての企業活動の場面で，リデュース（減少），リサイクル（再生），リユース（再使用）など環境保護に関する法令を遵守する．

1.13　個人情報保護
消費者との取引において得られた個人的な情報については，情報漏洩や不正な利用等のないように厳重に管理し保護する．

1.14　その他
以上の項目以外にも，例えば訪問販売等に関する法律や割賦販売法など，業種や業界によって様々な法令があるが，ここでは消費者に関連する要素が高い一般的な法令にとどめ，業種や業界固有の法令については記述を省略した．企業や組織の活動遂行にあたっては，当然のことながら，このような各種規制法令や業種や業界によって定められた様々な自主基準も遵守する．

2.　経済的責任
2.1　適正機能
製品やサービスについては消費者利益の視点に立ち，価格に見合う適正な機能を付することで消費者に経済的価値を提供する．

point of consumer benefits.

2.2 Fair Pricing

To aim to set fair prices for products and services that allow for fair profitability while endeavoring to cut their costs.

2.3 Provision of Rational and Economic Values

To provide consumers with products and services with rational and economic values that address their needs in terms of quality, performance, design, safety and usage, as well as fair functionality.

3. Ethical Commitment

3.1 Sincere Response and Grievance Procedures

To respond to various consumer queries, complaints or claims sincerely and promptly.

3.2 Making a Response Manual Available

To have a Response Manual pertaining to the process of responding consumer claims or complaints documented and maintained and publicized in and outside the company.

3.3 Receiving Needs and Complaints from Various Media

To open a customer consultation center (section) or office to actively respond to customer needs and complaints concerning products and services through a variety of media, including telephone, mail, questionnaires and the Internet (hereafter collectively "various media").

3.4 Factoring Consumer Opinions

To actively collect consumer opinions and views through various media and factor them into the making of products, services and stores.

3.5 Easy-to-View and Understand Marking and Content

To develop product or service documentation and advertising activi-

2.2 適正価格
製品やサービスの価格設定にあたっては，コスト低減に努力するとともに，適正利潤を得た適正価格の設定を目指す．

2.3 合理的で経済的な価値の提供
消費者ニーズを把握し，適正な機能以外にも品質，性能，デザイン，安全性，そして使用性などにおいて合理的で経済的な価値を提供する．

3. 倫理的責任

3.1 誠実な対応・苦情処理
消費者からの様々な問い合わせや不平・不満の申し出，苦情などには誠実かつ迅速に対応する．

3.2 応対マニュアルの整備
消費者からの問い合わせや苦情対応などに関する"応対マニュアル"を文書化・整備し，社内外に公表する．

3.3 多様なメディアによるニーズ・苦情の受付
お客様相談センター（室）や窓口などの部署を設けて，電話，手紙，アンケート，インターネットなどの多様なメディア（以下，多様なメディアという）を通じて，製品やサービスに関する消費者ニーズや苦情申し出に積極的に対応する．

3.4 消費者の意見の反映
多様なメディアを通じて，消費者の意見や声を積極的に収集し，製品やサービス，店づくりに反映させる．

3.5 見やすく分かりやすい表示・内容
製品やサービスの説明書，広告宣伝活動については，消費者に見やすく分か

ties in a format that is easy for consumers to view and understand.

3.6 Quick and Appropriate Logistics

To endeavor to achieve fair and speedy physical distribution of products and services at reasonable costs with environmental concerns taken into account.

3.7 Disclosing Demerit Information

To disclose and publicize demerit information, such as that about products and services, to consumers through various media in a positive manner.

3.8 Consumer Participation-Oriented Management

To aim to implement consumer-oriented management to encourage consumer to take part in product making and shop operating programs.

3.9 Consumer Enlightenment Activities

To develop consumer enlightenment activities on products or services actively through the medium of seminars, lecture meetings and so forth.

3.10 After-Sale Services

To endeavor to provide sincere after-sale services on products or services from consumers' standpoint once they are sold.

4. Community Commitment

4.1 Social Contribution

To promote enlightenment activities for social contributions and global environment conservation through the medium of seminars, lecture meetings and so forth in support of both communities and consumers.

4.2 Supporting the Creation of a Barrier-Free Society

To allow for socially vulnerable people, such as the physically dis-

りやすい表示・内容とする．

3.6 迅速かつ適切な物流活動
製品やサービスの提供にあたっては，環境問題に配慮しつつ合理的コストで適正かつ迅速な物流活動を心がける．

3.7 デメリット情報の開示
多様なメディアを通じて，製品やサービスに関するデメリット情報も積極的に消費者に開示・公表する．

3.8 消費者参加指向の経営
消費者がものづくりや店舗運営に参画できるように，消費者に密着した経営を目指す．

3.9 消費者啓発活動
セミナーや講演会等を通じて，製品やサービスに関する消費者啓発活動を積極的に行う．

3.10 アフターサービス
製品やサービスの販売後は，消費者の立場になって誠実なアフターサービスを心がける．

4. 社会貢献的責任
4.1 社会貢献の啓発活動
社会や消費者の支援のために，セミナーや講演会等を通じて社会貢献，地球環境保全活動に対する啓発活動を推進する．

4.2 バリアフリー社会の構築支援
製品やサービスの開発などにあたっては，障害者や高齢者，子供など社会的

abled, senior citizens and children, in the development of products and services to contribute to the creation of a barrier-free society.

4.3 Donation Participation Activities

To develop donation participation activities aimed at preventing and curing diseases and relieving socially vulnerable people to contribute to the growth of the communities.

弱者の救済・支援に配慮し，バリアフリー社会の実現に寄与する．

4.3　寄付金協賛型活動
　疾病の予防・治療活動や，弱者救済のための寄付金協賛型活動を展開し，社会に貢献する．

II. Suppliers and Customers

1. Legal Responsibility

1.1 Complying with Laws and Regulations

To comply with the applicable laws and regulations, including the Antitrust Law, in dealing with all suppliers and customers on the principle of free competition, adhere to fair trade practices and build trade relations of mutual profit.

1.2 Ban on Unfair Trade

To refrain from soliciting unfair trade from suppliers and customers by dealing with all with fair, impartial and sincere attitudes, and from infringing on intellectual property rights, such as patents, trademark rights, copyrights, utility model rights, and design rights.

1.3 Ban on Bid Rigging

To keep bidders from forming rigging in tendering for the procurement of products and services.

1.4 Ban on Abuse of Dominant Bargaining Positions

To maintain mutually fair trade relations with suppliers in terms of product quality, pricing, delivery times and so forth, and refrain from giving discriminative treatment to suppliers or abusing dominant bargaining positions based on company size differences.

1.5 Ban on Reciprocal Dealings

To maintain co-existence and co-prosperity with suppliers and customers and refrain from conducting reciprocating trade in violation of fair market rules.

1.6 Ban on Embarrassing Subcontractors

To refrain from any conduct that could be thought of as an act of subcontractor embarrassment, such as rejecting the receipt of deliveries

II. 取引先

1. 法的責任

1.1 関連法令等の遵守

すべての取引先との間で，自由な競争原理に基づき，独占禁止法等関連する法令を遵守し，適正な商習慣に従い，相互に適正な利益をあげられる取引関係を確立・維持する．

1.2 不公正な取引の禁止

すべての取引先に対し，公正・公平で誠実な態度で接し，不公正な取引を誘引するような行為は行わない．また，取引先独自の権利（知的財産権，特許権，実用新案権，商標権，意匠権等）を侵害しない．

1.3 談合の禁止

取引先からの製品やサービスの調達に際し入札を行う場合には，参加者が談合することのないように統制する．

1.4 優越的地位の濫用の禁止

企業と取引先が相互に適切な品質，価格，納期など公正な取引関係を維持する．企業規模の大小を背景とするような差別的な取扱い，優越的地位の濫用を行わない．

1.5 互恵取引の禁止

企業と取引先が相互の共存共栄を維持するとともに，公正な市場ルールに反するような互恵取引を行わない．

1.6 下請けいじめの禁止

下請会社との取引に際しては，契約済み製品の受領拒否，代金の支払遅延や減額，不当な返品，強制購入行為など下請けいじめと見られるような行為は行

on contract, delaying the payment of bills or cutting on the bills, returning deliveries for undue reasons, and forcing purchases, in dealing with subcontractors.

1.7 Ban on Infringing on Trade Secrets

To make resort to legally valid means and methods in collecting information about suppliers and customers with care not to infringe upon their trade secrets.

1.8 Ban on Urging Compulsory Adherence to Company Standards

To refrain from urging suppliers and customers to adhere to company standards only in jointly developing products with them, but try to create standards of mutual profit.

1.9 Ban on Receiving Improper Rebates

To refrain from receiving improper kickbacks and rebates from suppliers through dumping or padding in an effort to boost mutual trade amounts.

1.10 Complying with International Codes

To comply with ISO standards and international codes urged by the global society, such as those pertaining to human rights, labor and environments, in dealing with suppliers and customers operating globally.

1.11. Ban on Bribery, Excessive Gift Giving, and Entertainment

To refrain from conducting any act of forcing private profits and interests (such as money, commodities and services) and bribery, and from a mutual, excessive gift giving or entertainment in violation of the common sense.

1.12 Ban on Corruption

To refrain from conducting any act of bribery or profit sharing with foreign civil servants, such as officers and staffs for foreign govern-

わない．

1.7 企業秘密侵害の禁止

取引先に関する情報収集に際しては，法的に適正な手段・方法による収集に徹し，相手の企業情報を侵害しないよう行動する．

1.8 自社規格の強制使用要請の禁止

取引先と協力して製品等を開発する場合には，相互に利益になるような規格を構築し，自社の規格使用だけを強制することを行わない．

1.9 不正な割戻しの禁止

企業と取引先が，相互の取引額などの増大を意図した不正な低価格や水増し価格による不正なキックバック，割戻し等を行わない．

1.10 国際基準の遵守

国際的な取引先との関係では，ISO の各種規格をはじめ，人権，労働，環境など，国際社会から要請されている国際基準を遵守する．

1.11 賄賂・過度な贈答・接待の禁止

取引先との関係では，私的な利益，便益（金銭，物品，サービスなど）や賄賂を強制するような行為を行わない．また，相互に社会常識に反するような，過度な贈答・接待を行わない．

1.12 腐敗防止の禁止

国際取引において，外国政府・地方公共団体の役職員など，外国公務員等に対し贈賄行為や利益供与行為は行わない．

ments or municipalities, in international trade transaction.

1.13 Elimination of Inappropriate Payment Methods

To reject any method of payment that could assist in money laundering.

2. Economic Responsibility

2.1 Maintaining Proper Profitability

To manage the whole supply chains of products and services to gain consumer satisfaction together with suppliers and customers, thereby giving full consideration to both their safety and quality while maintaining proper profits.

2.2 Proper Tax Obligation

To fully appreciate the tax obligation as corporate taxpayers together with suppliers and customers and collaborate with them in cost and profit sharing.

2.3 Enhancing Mutual Levels of Technology

To endeavor to enhance the levels of technology to deliver products and services in collaboration with suppliers and customers.

2.4 Mutual Accountability

To fulfill mutual accountability with reference to correct data with regard to the products and services that are delivered to customers.

3. Ethical Commitment

3.1 Mutual Trust

To build a relationship of trust with suppliers and customers to prompt mutual sustainable development through smooth business communication with them in the supply chain.

1.13　不適切な支払方法の排除

不正な資金洗浄（マネーロンダリング）に加担する可能性のある支払方法は受け入れない．

2.　経済的責任
2.1　適正利益の維持

企業と取引先は相互にサプライチェーン全体を管理しながら，消費者が満足するように，製品やサービスの安全性及び品質に十分配慮し，適正な利益を確保できるような諸条件を決定する．

2.2　適正な納税義務

企業と取引先が相互に，企業として適正に納税する義務を十分認識し，費用・利益の配分に協力する．

2.3　相互の技術水準の向上

企業と取引先が相互に，協調して製品やサービスが提供できるよう技術水準の向上に努める．

2.4　相互の説明責任

取引先へ提供する製品やサービスについては，常に正確なデータに基づき相互の説明責任を果たす．

3.　倫理的責任
3.1　相互信頼

サプライチェーンの中での取引先との業務上の円滑なコミュニケーションなどによって，信頼関係を構築し，相互に持続可能な発展を促進する．

3.2 Equal Partnership

To pursue mutually sustainable business growth in developing quality product and services by partnering with suppliers and customers on an equal, transparent and fair basis.

3.3 Prompting Suppliers and Customers for Legal Compliance

To encourage suppliers and customers to normalize their work routines for compliance with relevant laws and regulations.

3.4 Heeding Global Environment Conservation

To promote corporate activities both at home and abroad to deliver fully eco-friendly products and services in partnership with suppliers and customers.

3.5 Mutual Trade Based on Social Trust

To conduct fair and sincere mutual transactions with suppliers and customers based on relationships of mutual trust with them and always treat them on a fair and impartial basis to conduct transactions in good faith under contract.

3.6 Respecting Human Rights

To endeavor to expedite mutual trade relationships with suppliers and customers in respect of the human rights of the workers involved.

3.7 Respecting Independent Management

To respect the independent corporate management stance of suppliers and customers and always approach in good faith.

3.8 Discretion in Entertainment and Gift Giving

To refrain from entertainment and gift-giving deeds that could have an irrational effect on trade in accordance with accepted business practices.

3.9 Ban on Conflict of Interests

To refrain from conducting inappropriate business dealings with

3.2 対等なパートナー

取引先との関係は，対等なパートナーとして，常に透明かつ公正であることを目指し，良質な製品とサービスを開発して，お互いの持続的な事業の繁栄を目指す．

3.3 取引先への法令遵守を促進

取引先の活動に対しても，関係法令の遵守が図られるように，適正化を促す努力をする．

3.4 地球環境保全への配慮

企業と取引先が相互に，地球環境保全を十分配慮した製品やサービスの提供に努め，国内をはじめグローバルな企業活動を推進する．

3.5 社会の信頼に基づく相互取引

取引先としてお互いに信頼関係に基づき，公正で誠実な相互取引を行う．常に対等，公正な立場で接し，契約に従って誠実な取引を行う．

3.6 人権尊重

企業と取引先が相互に，働く人々の人権を尊重し，相互の取引関係が円滑に行われるように努める．

3.7 自主経営の尊重

取引先に対し，企業としての独自の経営姿勢を尊重し，常に誠意をもって対応する．

3.8 接待・贈答の慎重な対応

本来の取引に不合理な影響をもたらすおそれのある接待・贈答については，適正なビジネス慣習に従い，慎む．

3.9 利益相反の禁止

従業員・役員本人，また，その親戚縁者や親しい友人が所有・経営する取引

employees or officers or with the companies owned or run by their relatives or close friends of them.

3.10 Breaking Up Trade with Antisocial Groups and Organizations

To break up commercial dealings with antisocial groups or organizations decisively, regardless of whether such dealings are ordinary or not.

3.11 Promoting Disclosure of Information

To promote fair disclosure of information for mutual review by consumers. Comparisons with products or services from other groups, if necessary, should be conducted with reference to correct information, and endeavor to disclose information of interest to consumers even if it is disadvantageous.

3.12 Promoting Dialogs with Stakeholders

To promote holding dialogs with stakeholders, mutually with suppliers and customers, through various means, such as holding meetings, interviewing, conducting awareness surveys, and collecting suggested ideas.

4. Community Commitment

4.1 Promoting Cooperative Social Contribution Activities

To promote social contribution and conservative activities of global environment, such as cooperating in local activities, making fair monetary donations, making company facilities accessible, implementing clean environment programs and assisting people with disabilities, by working in conjunction with suppliers and customers to address social urges.

4.2 Supply Chain Activities

To address urges from stakeholders and thus live to the expectations

先に不適正な取引を行わない．

3.10 反社会的勢力・団体との取引根絶
　反社会的勢力・団体に対しては，通常の商取引であっても関係を絶ち，断固として対決する．

3.11 情報開示の促進
　企業と取引先が相互に，消費者から評価されるよう，適正に情報公開を推進する．他のグループの製品やサービスと比較が必要なときは，正確な情報をもとに行い，たとえ不利な情報であっても，消費者に必要なものは開示するように努める．

3.12 ステークホルダーとの対話の促進
　企業と取引先が相互に，ステークホルダーに対して，会合，インタビュー，意識調査，アイデア募集など，様々な方式を通じてステークホルダーとの対話を促進する．

4. 社会貢献的責任
4.1 協調的な社会貢献活動の推進
　社会の要請に対して，企業と取引先が相互に協調し本業を中心に，地域活動への協力，適正な寄付行為，会社施設の提供，環境クリーン行事や障害者支援活動への参加など社会貢献，地球環境保全活動を推進する．

4.2 サプライチェーンの活動
　取引先を包含するサプライチェーンを構築するなどして，ステークホルダー

of social trust, as by forming supply chains inclusive of the suppliers and customers.

4.3 Promoting Volunteerism in International Corporate Activities
To promote volunteerism in operating as a global corporation in full consideration of the histories, cultures and customs in the operating countries and regions, with aids and volunteerism being concentrated on economically disadvantaged countries and regions.

の要請に対応できるように協力して，社会の信頼にこたえる．

4.3 国際企業活動におけるボランティア活動の推進

グローバル企業として活動を行うに際しては，各国，各地域の歴史，文化，習慣など，それぞれの実情を十分考慮の上ボランティア活動を推進する．特に，経済的に恵まれない地域・国に対しては，援助やボランティア活動を集中させる．

III. Employees

1. Legal Responsibility

1.1 Concluding Employment Regulations and a Labor-Management Agreement

To establish employment regulations that provide for working conditions, such as working hours, holidays and breaks, how to determine and pay wages, service disciplines, and personnel matters, such as assignment, personnel relocation and retirement, and conclude a labor-management agreement consented by both the management and employees in connection with the employment regulations.

1.2 Complying with Service Disciplines

To comply with service disciplines employees are obliged to abide by in providing their services pursuant to a labor contract, such as in-house rules, regulations and notifications, orders and instructions, attendance and absence, office guidelines, dress code, morale code, safety and health, and facility management.

1.3 Confirming and Making Widely Known Employee Codes and Rules

To require managers and competent sections to fully understand the codes and regulations that employees need to abide by and make them expressly known to the employees.

1.4 Ban on Discriminative Employment

To refrain from discriminating employees at employment for reasons of any characteristics that do not relate to their job related criteria, such as nationality, race, gender, sexual orientation, age, origin, academic career, personal connections, and disabilities, and publicize employment information broadly to the public, through the Internet,

III. 従業員

1. 法的責任
1.1 就業規則・労使協定の締結

労働時間・休暇・休憩等の労働条件，賃金の決め方・払い方，服務規律，配置・異動・退職等の人事などの就業規則，さらにこれらに関連して経営者と従業員が同意した労使協定を定める．

1.2 服務規律の遵守
社内規則・規定・通達，命令・指示，出退勤，勤務心得，服装，風紀，安全衛生，施設管理など，従業員が労働契約に基づき労務を提供する場合に従うべき義務事項である服務規律を遵守する．

1.3 従業員関連法規・規則の確認，周知

従業員が守るべき関連法規，規則などを経営者や担当部署が十分に把握し，これらの内容を従業員に対して明確に周知する．

1.4 差別的採用の禁止
国籍，人種，性別，性的指向性，年齢，出身，学歴，縁戚関係，障害など個人の能力以外の項目で採用を差別化しない．また，採用に関する情報は，インターネットや就職雑誌などを通して広く一般に公表する．

employment journals and so forth.

1.5 Ban on Discriminative Personnel Management and Treatment

To refrain from giving discriminative personnel relocation or discriminative promotion or demotion to employees for reasons of their unfair labor practice, thought and creed, nationality, race, sex, sexual preference, age, origin, academic career, personal connection, disabilities and so forth, regardless of their job related criteria.

1.6 Protecting Personal Information

To refrain from making personal information on employees available to others or using or disclosing it without the employees' consent, without due reason, as by law.

1.7 Complying with Laws and Regulations for Working Hours, Holidays and Leaves

To set working hours for employees working overtime, on holidays, late at night, and on night and day duties pursuant to the Labor Standards law and grant them holidays and leaves, such as paid holidays, pre- and post- child birth holidays and special holidays.

1.8 Complying with Laws and Regulations for Wage Payment

To comply with the five rules of employee wage payment; cash payment (including bank transfer), direct payment to employees, payment in full amount, monthly payment, and payment on a fixed date, and pay overtime premium and extra wages, bonuses, retirement allowance and so forth in accordance with the employment regulations.

1.9 Promoting Equal Employment, and Ban on Sexual and Power Harassment

To refrain from discriminating employees by gender at their recruitment and employment, placement, promotion, education and training,

1.5 差別的な人事・処遇の禁止

従業員個人の能力とは関係なく，不当労働行為，思想信条，国籍，人種，性別，性的指向性，年齢，出身，学歴，縁戚関係，障害等に基づく差別的人事異動や，昇進・昇格の差別を行わない．

1.6 個人情報の保護

従業員の個人情報については，法令に基づくなどの正当な理由がある場合を例外として，本人の同意を得ることなく他に提供したり，利用・開示したりしない．

1.7 労働時間，休暇・休業に関する法令遵守

労働基準法に基づき，従業員の時間外・休日，深夜，宿日直などの労働時間を設定するとともに，有給休暇，産前産後休暇，特別休暇などの休暇・休業を付与する．

1.8 賃金の支払いに関する法令遵守

従業員への賃金の支払いでは，現金払い（振込含む），本人への直接払い，全額払い，毎月払い，一定期日支払いの五つの原則を遵守する．また，就業規則に基づき，残業賃金や割増賃金，賞与，退職金等を支払う．

1.9 男女雇用機会均等の推進，セクシャルハラスメント・パワーハラスメントの禁止

従業員の募集・採用，配置，昇進，教育訓練，福利厚生，定年・退職・解雇等において，性別による差別をしない．また，性別や職場内地位の違いによっ

welfare and benefit, age limits, retirement and dismissal and so forth, and prevent employees from being put at a disadvantage, such as dismissal, demotion, job relocation, and workplaces, because of their gender or differences of position level.

1.10 Ban on Child Labor and Forced Labor

To ban the labor of children short of the minimum working age and undue forced labor of employees against their will, because these labor practices infringe on fundamental human rights.

1.11 Responding to Dispatch Workers

To comply with the Worker Dispatch Law in dispatching workers, as by concluding a dispatch contract between the dispatching firm and the recipient firm.

1.12 Heeding Employee Safety and Health

To ensure employee safety and health in accordance with the Industrial Safety and Health Law and promote the formation of a comfortable workplace.

1.13 Responding to and Handling Occupational Disasters

To fully compare occupational disasters or accidents during travel to and from work as they occur with their past cases and provide necessary compensation to the affected employees.

1.14 Forming a Scheme of Compliance Promotion and Publicizing Related Information

To define the laws and regulations, and rules employees need to abide by to shape and maintain corporate growth and to establish and maintain a scheme of compliance to penetrate and sustain the spirit of integrity in a corporation.

て，従業員が解雇，降格，転勤，職場環境などの不利益を被ることを禁止する．

1.10 児童労働，強制労働の禁止

就業の最低年齢に達しない児童労働及び従業員の意思に反する不当な強制労働は，基本的人権を侵害することから禁止する．

1.11 労働者派遣への対応

労働者派遣を行う場合には，派遣会社と派遣労働者を受け入れる会社とが派遣契約を締結するなどの労働者派遣法を遵守する．

1.12 従業員の安全と健康に対する配慮

労働安全衛生法に基づき，従業員の安全と健康を確保するとともに，快適な職場環境の形成を促進する．

1.13 労働災害への対策・対応

業務災害，通勤災害が発生した際には，該当する先行事例を十分に照らし合わせ，その従業員に対して必要な補償を行う．

1.14 コンプライアンス推進体制の構築と関連情報の公開

企業の維持・発展のために従業員が遵守すべき法令・諸規則を明確にし，企業倫理を浸透，定着するためのコンプライアンス体制を確立するとともに，これらが常に守られているかを確認する．

2. Economic Responsibility

2.1 Sharing of Management Goals

To allow employees to share a firm notion of management goals and guidelines and set employee-specific targets necessary to achieve those goals.

2.2 Paying Fair Wages and Incentives

To pay enough wages for employees and their families to maintain a fair standard of living and give inventors and excellently performing employees valid, reasonable amounts of incentives.

2.3 Fair and Impartial Personnel Evaluation and Appropriate Personnel Transfer

To maintain a personnel rating system to give fair evaluations to employees' abilities, aptitude and performance, plus a self-assessment system, a system of management by objectives and so on, to provide an environment in which the employees can maximize their abilities at their own initiatives.

2.4 Appropriate Benefit Program and Measures

To maintain and provide a benefit program and measures to create a friendly environment in which employees find themselves easy to work.

2.5 Supporting Employee Education and Ability Development

To encourage employees in their efforts to acquire skills and know-how relevant to developing their abilities and creativity and self-develop themselves, provide them with opportunities for education and training to that end, and support their attendance to seminars, courses and other educational sessions.

2.6 Safe and Clean Workplace

To maintain a workplace that is designed to enhance employees' work

2. 経済的責任

2.1 経営目標の共有

企業全体の経営目標，経営方針を従業員としっかりと共有し，その目標達成のために必要な従業員一人ひとりの目標を明確に設定する．

2.2 妥当な賃金・報奨金の支給

従業員及びその家族が適正な生活水準を維持できるに足りる賃金を支払う．また，発明者や業績優秀な従業員に対して妥当性，納得性のある報奨金を支給する．

2.3 公平かつ公正な人事評価，適正な人事異動

従業員の能力・適性，業績を正当に評価する人事考課制度の整備とともに，自己申告制度，目標管理制度などによって，従業員が積極的に自らの能力を最大限に発揮できる環境を提供する．

2.4 妥当な福利厚生制度・施策

従業員に優しく，働きやすい福利厚生制度や施策を整備，提供する．

2.5 従業員教育，能力向上の支援

従業員個人の能力や創造性発揮のために，関連するスキル・ノウハウの習得や自己啓発を奨励し，教育・研修の場を設定したり，従業員が学習するためのセミナーや教育講座等の受講を支援したりする．

2.6 安全かつ清潔な職場環境

従業員の仕事の能率があがる職場環境を整備する．また，業務遂行の悪影響

efficiency, and improve on the workplace in a positive manner if it is likely to adversely affect the fulfillment of jobs.

2.7 Promotion Computerization

To allow key corporate information and management data to be shared as much as possible to promote information exchanges between employees and between different departments of the company.

2.8 Disclosing Corporate Information

To proactively publicize corporate information, such as financial positions, product information, services, organizations, IR (Investor Relations) and employment, in annual reports, homepages, corporate literature and so forth, and thereby ensure disclosure of corporate information to employees as well as external stakeholders.

3. Ethical Commitment

3.1 Respecting Individualities and Heeding Human Rights

To position employees to promote human-rights activities and hold dialogs with stakeholders and always to respect the employees' human rights, personalities and individualities.

3.2 Equality in the Workplace

To endeavor to always give fair treatment to employees working in the same company or in the same workplace without discriminating them on the basis of their membership or non-membership of a labor union and being a full-time or part-time employee, as well as their gender and job.

3.3 Making the Workplace and Employment Barrier-free

To maintain a workplace necessary to enable employees to promote the fulfillment of their jobs in a sound and efficient manner and also

になるような職場環境については積極的に改善していく．

2.7 情報化の推進
　企業の必要な情報や経営データを可能な限り共有化し，従業員相互間，部門間の情報交流を推進する．

2.8 企業情報の公開
　企業の財務内容，製品情報，サービス内容，組織，IR（Investor Relations：インベスター・リレーションズ），採用関連などの企業情報については，年報（アニュアルレポート），ホームページ，会社資料等を通して積極的に公開することによって，社外のステークホルダーのみならず，従業員への企業情報公開の徹底を図る．

3. 倫理的責任
3.1 個人の尊重，人権配慮
　人権活動を推進し，ステークホルダーとの対話を行う役割をもつ従業員を配置し，従業員一人ひとりの人権や人格，個性を常に尊重する．

3.2 職場における平等
　同じ企業，職場のなかでは，性別，職種などの違いはもちろん，労働組合加入の有無，正規従業員・非正規従業員の区別などに基づく差別的な対応を行わず，常に平等な対応を心がける．

3.3 職場環境及び雇用のバリアフリー
　従業員が健全かつ能率的に業務推進するために，十分な職場環境を整えるとともに，障害者が健常者と同様に就業できる環境づくりに配慮する．

endeavor to build an environment enabling people with disabilities to work the same way as do ordinary persons.

3.4 Supporting Childcare and Nursing Care Beyond Legal Requirements

To endeavor to improve and enhance, to the extent possible the support program designed to minimize the burden of employees involved in childcare or nursing care and enable them to maximize their abilities and competency.

3.5 Promoting Women and People with Disabilities Actively

To eliminate sexual discrimination and discrimination for people with disabilities in the workplace and positively introduce a corporate culture and programs to support these employees at work while making maximum use of their abilities.

3.6 Responding to Health Care and Mental Care

To emphasize and actively encourage the sound improvement of physical and mental conditions of employees to help the maximized their abilities.

3.7 Communication and Human Relations in the Workplace

To endeavor to activate communication across the company, as by messages directly transmitted to employees from the management at its initiative and holding talks with the employees, and forge a corporate culture in which employees can respect each other's stances.

3.8 Realization of a Balance between Work and Life

To actively support the realization of both full private life – in terms of home, health, study and self-improvement – and good work.

3.9 Exchanging with Other Stakeholders, such as Consumers, Suppliers, Customers and Local Communities

To actively arrange for chances and opportunities for employees to get

3.4 法令を上回る育児・介護支援

育児・介護に携わる従業員の負担を極力軽減し，能力・活力を最大限に引き出せるよう，企業は可能な限りの支援制度の充実・拡充に心がける．

3.5 女性や障害者の積極登用
職場における性差別や障害者に対する差別を排除することはもちろんのこと，これらの従業員の活躍を支援する企業風土・制度を積極的に導入し，その能力の最大限の活用を図る．

3.6 ヘルスケア・メンタルケアの対応
従業員の肉体・精神の健全な発展を重視するとともに，その成長を積極的に促すことによって，個々人の能力の最大限の発揮を心がける．

3.7 職場内のコミュニケーション，人間関係
経営者から率先して従業員にメッセージを流したり，対話を行ったりし，会社全体としてのコミュニケーションの活性化に努める．また，お互いの立場を尊重して相手を思いやる心をもてるような職場風土を形成する．

3.8 ワークライフバランスの実現
従業員が家庭や健康，自己研鑽などの充実した私生活と仕事との両立ができるように積極的に支援する．

3.9 消費者，取引先，地域社会など他のステークホルダーとの交流

従業員が消費者，取引先，地域社会などのステークホルダーと接する場や機

into touch with stakeholders, such as consumers, suppliers, customers and local communities, and forge an organizational culture in which the employees can hold dialogs with the stakeholders in good faith.

3.10 Rules of Political and Religious Activities

To respect the political creed and religious belief of each individual employee but not to permit employees to stage political and religious activities in the company as a rule.

3.11 Responding Sincerely to Whistle Blowing and Illicit Behavior Reports Speedily

To strictly observe secrecy obligations, such as anonymity, for employees coming up with questions, seeking consultation and sending notifications about code compliance, in-house rules, corporate ethics and so forth to keep them harmless and respond to the opinions and information submitted by them in good faith, returning appropriate responses to them.

3.12 Disclosing Negative Information

To release information relevant to employees quickly and accurately even though it may have a negative impact on the company.

4. Community Commitment

4.1 Encouraging Volunteerism

To support and encourage volunteerism by employees by granting volunteer holidays to facilitate their work or disseminating announcement for volunteers to employees.

4.2 Taking Active Part in Local Community Activities

To encourage employees to take active part in community festivals and events and support their participation positively.

会を積極的に設定し，従業員が誠意をもってステークホルダーと対話できるような組織風土を構築する．

3.10 政治・宗教活動のルール
個人の政治的信条や信仰する宗教を尊重するものの，企業内での政治・宗教活動は原則として許可しない．

3.11 内部告発・不祥事への誠意ある迅速な対応

従業員から法令遵守，社内規則，企業倫理などに対する疑問，相談，通報等を寄せられた際には，その発信者が不利益を被らないよう匿名性や守秘義務を厳守するとともに，そこで寄せられた意見，内容に対して誠意をもって対応し，必要に応じて発信者に対する的確な回答を行う．

3.12 マイナス情報の開示
従業員に対して必要な情報については，自社にとってマイナスの影響がある場合であっても迅速，かつ正確に提供する．

4. 社会貢献的責任
4.1 ボランティア活動の奨励
従業員がボランティア活動をしやすいよう，必要に応じてボランティア休暇を設定したり，ボランティアを募る案内を従業員に提供したりするなどの奨励・支援を行う．
4.2 地域社会活動への積極的な参加
従業員が地域活動やイベントに積極的に参加することを奨励するとともに，積極的に支援する．

4.3 Contributing to Cultures, Arts and Sports

To encourage employees to take active part in cultural, artistic and sport activities.

4.4 Contributing to Education

To encourage employees to work as lecturers in school education, seminars and other sessions as a clue to developing possible human resources.

4.5 Matching Gifts

To promote the charity or gift activities through the united effort of the company and the organization as its employees conduct volunteer activities.

4.6 Supporting Environmental Conservation Activities

To give active support to employees in their effort to tackle environmental conservation activities, such as energy saving, giving top priority to those efforts seeking to preserve the global environment for generations to come.

4.7 Promoting Linkage with NPOs/NGOs

To support holding active dialogs with NPOs and NGOs to facilitate the work of employees in pursuit of social contribution and conservative activities of global environment.

4.8 Providing Information about Social Contribution Activities

To define the stakeholders that are targeted by employees in pursuit of social contribution and conservative activities of global environment and publicize them broadly to the general public, including the employees, in CSR Reports, Sustainability Reports and so forth, and support the employees to respond in good faith to opinions and views received in response to such publicized information.

4.3 文化・芸術・スポーツへの貢献

従業員が文化・芸術・スポーツ活動に積極的に参加することを奨励する．

4.4 教育関係への貢献

従業員が学校教育やセミナー等の講師を務めることを奨励し，企業にとっての将来的な人材育成を図る．

4.5 マッチング・ギフト

従業員がボランティア活動を行うにあたって，企業や組織も一帯になってチャリティーやギフト活動を推進する．

4.6 環境保全活動への支援

従業員がリサイクル，省エネルギーなど環境保全活動を取り組むにあたっては積極的に支援する．支援にあたっては，次世代に引き継ぐ貴重な地球環境を保全する活動を最優先に行う．

4.7 NPO/NGO との連携促進

従業員の行う社会貢献，地球環境保全活動については，NPO/NGO との積極的な対話をサポートし，効果的な活動となるように努める．

4.8 社会貢献活動に関する情報提供

従業員が，社会貢献，地球環境保全活動などの実施にあたっては，その対象とするステークホルダーを明確にし，CSR 報告書やサステナビリティ報告書等を通して，従業員も含めて広く一般に公開する．また，これらの公開情報に寄せられた意見，要望等に対しては従業員が誠意をもって対応できるよう支援する．

IV. Shareholders and Investors

1. Legal Responsibility

1.1 Legal Compliance

To act on the prime principle of complying with all applicable laws and regulations pertaining to shareholders and investors, including the Commercial Code, the Securities Exchange Law and Generally Accepted Accounting Principles, from a corporate governance standpoint.

1.2 Ban on Insider Trading

To refrain from any stock trading practice that is deemed insider trading and, if sensitive information about insider trading is obtained, discontinue trading until the information is publicized.

1.3 Ban on Illicit Trading

To refrain from selling, buying and otherwise trading stocks and securities by manners that are generally accepted illicit under normal social conventions, such as a fraudulent practice.

1.4 Ban on Rigging and Illicit Operations for Stabilizing Stock Market Prices

To refrain from rigging stock prices in the company's favor or perform operations that attempt to stabilize stock prices illegally without due notification or procedures.

1.5 Appropriate Accounting Procedures

To comply with the Tax Law and the Generally Accepted Accounting Principles to keep financial and tax accounting accurate and reliable and also with relevant laws and regulations and in-house rules to prevent illicit or manipulated accounting.

IV. 株主・投資家

1. 法的責任

1.1 法令遵守

　企業活動においてコーポレートガバナンスの視点から株主・投資家にかかわる商法や証券取引法，企業会計原則など，あらゆる法令を遵守することを基本的な理念として掲げて行動する．

1.2 インサイダー取引の禁止

　インサイダー取引に該当するおそれのある株取引は一切行わない．また，インサイダー取引に関する重要情報を入手した場合には，その情報が公開されるまで取引を禁止する．

1.3 不公正取引の禁止

　株式及び有価証券の売買その他の取引は，詐欺的行為など，社会通念上不正と認められる手段を用いて行わない．

1.4 相場操縦と違法な株価安定操作の禁止

　株価を人為的に操縦し，自社に有利な株価を作り出したり，正式な届出や手続きを経ない不公正な株価安定操作を行わない．

1.5 適正な会計処理

　財務・税務会計の正確性，信頼性を確保するため，税法や企業会計原則を遵守し，適正な会計処理を行う．法令や社内規定を遵守し，不適正な会計処理は行わない．

1.6 Protecting Personal and Group Information

To mange diverse information pertaining to individuals and groups who are shareholders in a proper manner to prevent their external leakages.

2. Economic Responsibility

2.1 Maintaining Financial Soundness, and Paying Taxes

To build a sound financial positions and pay due taxes in accordance with relevant laws and regulations to contribute to the growth of the communities.

2.2 Paying Shareholder Dividends

To complete due payment of shareholder dividends by acting to pursue a fair and impartial sharing of profits through proper corporate activities that are primarily committed to fulfilling social responsibilities.

2.3 Heeding Continual Corporate Growth

To heed continual corporate growth, as by keeping appropriate retained earnings, to maintain financial soundness.

2.4 Emphasizing Strategic Planning

To develop and carry into action strategic plans worked out from not only short-term and financial but longer-term and social standpoints with industry-unique characteristics taken into account.

2.5 Reforming Technologies Continually

To develop continual technological innovations compatible with the social environment in continuous pursuit of the corporate growth.

2.6 Implementing Crisis Management

To implement thorough crisis management by properly managing risks hidden in corporate activities to avoid a huge degradation of the

1.6　個人・団体情報の保護

株主である個人や団体にかかわる各種情報を適切に管理し，外部への漏洩を防止する．

2.　経済的責任

2.1　財務の健全性確保・納税

健全な財務体質を確保し，定められた法令に則り，然るべき納税を行うことで社会の発展に貢献する．

2.2　株主配当の実施

社会的責任への配慮を前提とした適切な企業活動を通じて，利益の公平・公正な分配を目指して行動し，適切な株主配当を実施する．

2.3　継続的な事業発展への配慮

財務の健全性を確保するため，適切な内部留保を実施するなど，継続的な事業発展に配慮する．

2.4　戦略計画の重視

業界特有の事情を勘案した上で，短期的・財務的観点だけでなく，中長期的・社会的観点にも配慮した戦略計画を立案し実践する．

2.5　継続的な技術革新

社会環境に配慮した継続的な技術革新を展開し，事業の発展に向けた努力を続ける．

2.6　危機管理の実施

企業活動のリスクを適切に管理し，企業価値の莫大な損失を招くことがないように危機管理を徹底する．

corporate value.

3. **Ethical Commitment**

3.1 **Installing Points of Contact with Shareholders and Investors**

To install points of contact with shareholders and investors, such as web sites, CSR reports, annual reports, to maintain positive two-way communication to promote understanding in the corporate activities from the shareholders and investors and gain insight into their needs to aid in the implementation of upcoming corporate activities.

3.2 **Responding to Fair and Transparent IR**

To develop fair and transparent IR activities at all times to augment management transparency and carry out continuous IR activities from longer standpoints to consolidate trust from shareholders and investors.

3.3 **Environmental and Social Reporting**

To promote the active disclosure of environmental and social, as well as financial, information to convey the diversity of corporate approaches in the social aspects of business to shareholders and investors.

3.4 **Presenting Environmental and Social Costs**

To positively disclose environmental and social costs involved in the implementation of corporate activities to invite understanding in their social aspects from shareholders and investors.

3.5 **Maintaining Corporate Reliability through Corporate Governance**

To spell out policy for corporate governance and get them fully understood to enhance the transparency and impartiality of management and maintain reliability in management as a whole.

3. 倫理的責任
3.1 株主・投資家との接点の設置
　ホームページや CSR 報告書，年報（アニュアルレポート）など，株主・投資家との接点を設置し，積極的な双方向のコミュニケーションを通じて，株主・投資家に対する企業活動への理解を促進するとともに，株主・投資家ニーズを把握し，企業活動に役立てる．

3.2 公正・透明な IR への対応
　常に公正で透明な IR 活動を展開し経営の透明性を高めるとともに，中長期的視点にたった持続的な IR 活動を実現することで，投資家・株主の信頼確保を目指し行動する．

3.3 環境・社会性報告の実施
　財務面に加えて，環境・社会面での情報開示を積極的に推進し，事業の社会的側面にかかわる多様な取組みについて株主・投資家に伝達する．

3.4 環境・社会コストの提示
　企業活動にかかわる環境・社会コストを積極的に開示することで，事業の社会的側面に関する株主・投資家の理解を得る．

3.5 コーポレートガバナンスによる企業の信頼性の確保

　コーポレートガバナンスに関する方針を明示・徹底し，経営の透明性・公平性を高めるとともに，経営全体に対する信頼性を確保する．

4. **Community Commitment**

4.1 **Heeding the Society and Environment**

To predict the possible social and environmental impacts of corporate activities and put into action measures designed to minimize the impacts with shareholders' and investors' opinions and advice taken into account.

4.2 **Sincere Corporate Stances**

To maintain consistency in organizational behavior in making every management decision and take positive interest in suggestions received from external sources from social standpoints, responding to them in a sincere corporate stance at all times.

4.3 **Developing Social Contribution Activities**

To actively develop social contribution activities to consolidate social trust and enhance the brand value.

4.4 **Promoting CSR Activities**

To promote CSR activities actively to place an effort to be integrated into the various SRI (Socially Responsible Investment) funds and thus to enhance to he corporate value and live up to shareholders' expectations.

4. 社会貢献的責任
4.1 社会や環境への配慮
　企業活動によって生じる社会的影響を事前に予測し，株主や投資家の意見やアドバイスも積極的に取り入れた上で，社会や環境への影響を最小限に抑えるための適切な対策を実施する．

4.2 誠実な企業姿勢
　あらゆる経営判断において，組織行動の一貫性を確保するとともに，社会的観点に基づく外部からの指摘に対して積極的に関心をもち，これらに常に誠実な企業姿勢で対応する．

4.3 社会貢献活動の展開
　社会貢献活動を積極的に展開し，社会的信頼の確立に努めるとともにブランド価値を高める．

4.4 CSR活動の推進
　CSR活動を積極的に推進し，各種SRI (Socially Responsible Investment：社会的責任投資) ファンドへの組入れを目指すことで，企業価値の向上と株主の期待にこたえていく．

V. Local Communities and Global Environment

1. Legal Responsibility

1.1 Maintaining Safety in Local Communities

To comply with all governing laws and regulations relating to fire prevention, architecture, security and traffic safety in conducting corporate activities to maintain safety in the local communities.

1.2 Complying with Environmental Standards and Implementing Maintenance Measures

To put into action various measures aimed at maintaining the health of local residents and preserving their living environment in compliance with the environmental standards set by the nation and communities.

1.3 Disposing of Waste Properly

To control and dispose of the waste arising from the implementation of corporate activities properly in accordance with prescribed standards.

1.4 Using Cyclically Reusable Resources

To put cyclically reusable resources arising from the implementation of corporate activities to reuse or recycle them in accordance with prescribed standards.

1.5 Disclosing Information about Chemical Substances

To have an insight into the volumes of the chemical substances, controlled as being harmful to local residents and the ecosystems, that are emitted to the air and water, and register and report that information in an appropriate manner.

1.6 Forming an Acceptable Landscape

To create a pleasant, living environment and build an artistic, elegant

V. 地域社会・地球環境

1. 法的責任

1.1 地域社会の安全確保

企業活動にあたっては，消防，建築に関する規制法令，治安，交通安全に関する法令等を遵守し，地域社会の安全確保を図る．

1.2 環境基準の遵守と保全対策の実施

国及び地域で定められた環境基準を遵守し，地域の人々の健康維持及び生活環境の保全を図るための各種対策を実施する．

1.3 廃棄物の適正な処理

企業活動において発生した廃棄物については，定められた基準に従って適正に管理・処理する．

1.4 循環資源の活用

企業活動において利用・発生する循環資源については，定められた基準に従って再生利用又は再資源化する．

1.5 化学物質に関する情報公開

地域の人々や生態系に有害で規制対象となる化学物質については，大気や水への排出量を把握するとともに，その情報を適切に報告・公表する．

1.6 良好な景観の形成

良好な景観の形成にかかわる法令・規制を遵守し，潤いのある豊かな生活環

society in compliance with the relevant laws and regulations that are committed to forming an acceptable landscape, thereby aiming to form an individualistic and vital local community.

1.7 Ban on Bribing Civil Servants

To refrain from gifting and entertaining civil servants with a view to drawing illicit profits or the like.

1.8 Others

To comply with international rules and local laws and regulations in conducting global corporate activities to help conserve the environments of the local communities, maintain the safety of the local communities, foster sound growth of the local economies and communities, promote public welfare and so forth.

2. Economic Responsibility

2.1 Proper Tax Payment

To duly pay the taxes that are levied on the implementation of corporate activities and the resultant products in accordance with international rules, Generally Accepted Accounting Procedures, relevant tax laws and regulations, community's ordinances and so forth.

2.2 Contributing to Sound Growth of Local Economies and Communities

To comply with relevant urban planning laws, and regulations relevant to location and business activities and so forth while implementing corporate activities, such as in locating buildings and facilities of factories and stores, to contribute to the sound growth of the local economies and communities.

境の創造及び芸術的で情緒ある社会の実現を図るとともに，ひいては個性的で活力ある地域社会の実現を目指す．

1.7 公務員に対する贈賄の禁止

公務員に対しては，不当な利益等の取得を目的とする贈答・接待を行わない．

1.8 その他

国際的な企業活動にあたっては，国際ルールや現地の法令を遵守し，事業を行う地域社会の環境保全や社会の安全の確保，地域経済・社会の健全な発展，公共の福祉増進等を図る．

2. 経済的責任

2.1 適正な納税

企業活動及びその成果等に対して課される税金については，国際ルールや会計処理及び税に関する諸法令，地域の条例等に基づき，適正に納める．

2.2 地域経済・社会の健全な発展への寄与

工場・店舗などの建物・施設等の立地及び企業活動にあたっては，都市計画にかかわる法令，各種立地・事業規制にかかわる法令等を遵守し，地域経済・社会の健全な発展に寄与する．

2.3 Management Contributing to Self-Sustained Growth of Local Communities

To intensify cooperative ties with local enterprises to contribute to the furtherance of local industries and endeavor not only to create employment but also to localize management so as to develop corporate activities tailored to specific local needs.

3. Ethical Commitment

3.1 Disclosing Information Properly and Timely

To disclose corporate information, as well as information pertaining to environmental and social safety, in a proper and timely manner to maintain transparency in corporate management, thereby fulfilling the obligation of accountability to the local communities and winning their understanding and trust.

3.2 Promoting Dialogs with Local Communities

To promote positive two-way communication with the local communities, including dialogs, to seek coexistence with them and develop corporate activities that address their expectations and urges and that could lead to the sound growth of the local economies, as well as local communities.

3.3 Confronting Antisocial Groups and Organizations

To declare firm resolutions in and outside the company to decisively eliminate antisocial groups or organizations that threaten the order and security of the civil society and tackle them by working in conjunction with trade associations and local enterprises and collaborating with the police to counter threats.

2.3 地域社会の自立的な発展に貢献する経営

地域企業との協力関係を緊密化し,地域産業の育成に貢献するとともに,雇用の確保はもとより,経営の地域化に努め,地域のニーズにあった企業活動を展開する.

3. 倫理的責任
3.1 適時適切な情報開示

地域社会への説明責任を果たし,その理解と信頼を得るため,環境や社会の安全にかかわる情報はもとより,企業情報を適時適切に開示し,事業運営に関する透明性を確保する.

3.2 地域社会との対話の促進

地域社会との共生を図り,地域社会の期待や要請にこたえ,地域経済・社会の健全な発展につながる企業活動を展開すべく,対話活動をはじめとする双方向のコミュニケーションを積極的に実施する.

3.3 反社会的勢力・団体との対決姿勢

市民社会の秩序や安全に脅威を与える反社会的勢力・団体に対しては,断固として排除する姿勢を明確に社内外に宣言する.業界団体や地域企業と連携し排除に取り組むとともに,威嚇(いかく)には,警察等と連携するなどして,毅然と対抗する.

3.4 Setting Voluntary Standards and Goals for Environmental Conservation Activities

To set voluntary standards and goals that are more demanding than are legal requirements from viewpoints of environmental conservation and social safety assurance and work positively to achieve these goals and to create and develop a scheme of management to achieve these goals.

3.5 Deploying Businesses in Respect of Local Cultures and Customs

To understand the social circumstances of a targeted region before deploying businesses to pay full heed to its cultures, practices and landscape.

4. Community Commitment

4.1 Supporting Social Contribution Activities

To take a strategic approach to conducting social contribution and conservative activities of global environment as a scheme of business investment for achieving sustainable growth, giving positive support to those activities that could lead to long-term profitability, such as better corporate reputation and the development of human resources.

4.2 Conducting Acts of Donation

To make positive donations to those organizations working to resolve the various problems encountered in the local communities from a viewpoint of giving monetary assistance to them.

4.3 Encouraging and Supporting Volunteering Employees

To encourage and support employees volunteering to resolve the various problems encountered in the local communities from a viewpoint of giving human resource assistance to them and to implement volun-

3.4 環境保全に向けた自主基準・目標の設定

環境保全や社会の安全を確保する観点から，法令等の基準を上回る自主基準・目標を設定し，その達成に向け積極的に取り組む．取組みにあたっては，マネジメント推進体制を適宜構築する．

3.5 地域社会の文化・慣習等を尊重した事業展開

事業を展開するにあたっては，当該地域の社会事情を理解し，その文化や慣習，景観に十分配慮した活動を行う．

4. 社会貢献的責任
4.1 社会貢献活動の支援
企業が実施する社会貢献，地球環境保全活動については，持続可能な発展のための企業活動の投資として戦略的に取り組み，イメージアップ，人材育成など自社の長期的な利益に結びつくような活動に対して積極的に支援する．

4.2 寄付活動の実施等
地域社会の諸課題の解決に向けた各種活動・取組みを，金銭的に支援する観点から，当該活動・取組みを実施する組織に対し，積極的に寄付を行う．

4.3 従業員のボランティア活動の奨励・支援
地域社会の諸課題の解決に向けた各種活動・取組みを，人的に支援する観点から，従業員のボランティア活動を積極的に奨励・支援する．支援にあたっては，ボランティア休暇制度等の諸支援制度を適宜導入する．

teer support programs, such as a volunteer holiday plan, as appropriate to support them.

4.4 Formulating Voluntary Programs

To take positive advantage of managerial resources in locating plants and other facilities, formulating voluntary programs, dispatching officers and employees, instituting corporate foundations, disseminating know-how and so forth from viewpoints of resolving various problems encountered in the local communities and encouraging their promotion or sustained growth.

4.5 Fostering NPOs/NGOs and Intensifying Partnership

To provide NPOs and NGOs working to cope with social issues, including environmental concerns with physical and technical, as well as financial, support that adds the technical expertise of business persons to their administration, and conduct various programs jointly with them, such as those for gaining access to the facilities owned by companies out of the recognition of the significance of their activities.

4.6 Coping with Natural Protection

To cope with the goal of natural protection activities, including the conservation of the diversity of living things, out of the notion that coexistence with diverse living things brings human beings a wealth living environment.

4.7 Supporting Humanity Respect Education

To provide positive support to humanity respect education to help future generations take interest in the problems and tasks of the communities, such as environmental conservation, and develop a sense of awareness and behavior to send a sound global environment and a human society to evolving generations.

4.4 自主プログラムの策定等

地域社会の諸課題を解決し,その振興や持続的な発展を図る観点から,自らの経営資源を積極的に生かし,立地はもとより,自主プログラムの策定や,役員・従業員の派遣,企業財団の設立,ノウハウの提供などを実施する.

4.5 NPO/NGO の育成,パートナーシップの強化

環境問題をはじめとする社会的課題への取組みに対する NPO/NGO の役割の重要性を認識し,資金的支援にとどまらず,企業人の専門性やノウハウを NPO/NGO の運営に生かす人的協力や情報提供,技術支援,並びに企業が保有する施設利用の便益提供等の多様な支援やプログラムの共同実施を行う.

4.6 自然保護への取組み

人類にとって多様な生物が共存することが豊かな生活環境をもたらすものであることを認識し,生物の多様性の保全を含めた自然保護活動に,積極的に取り組む.

4.7 人間尊重教育の支援

未来を担う世代に環境をはじめとする社会の問題・課題に関心をもってもらうとともに,健全な地球環境・人類社会を将来に引き継いでいくための意識や行動を育むための人間尊重教育を,積極的に支援する.

VI. Competitors

1. **Legal Responsibility**

1.1 **Complying with National Antitrust or Competition Laws and Other Relevant Laws and Regulations**

To compete with competitors in a fair and legal manner in compliance with local antitrust laws or competition laws.

1.2 **Ban on Private Monopoly**

To refrain from conducting any act of private monopoly that inappropriately interferes with the corporate activities of competitors or drives them out of market, as by boycotting.

1.3 **Ban on Unfair Trade Restrictions**

To refrain from forming cartels or from rigging bids, as by deciding, maintaining or raising prices jointly with other firms in the same line of business or with trade associations, agreeing on production or sales quantities, designating prospective successful bidders, or otherwise posing unfair trade restrictions.

1.4 **Ban on Unfair Trade Practices**

To refrain from conducting any unfair trade practice that interferes with competitors' business, such as dumping.

1.5 **Ban on Giving Bribes to Public Servants**

To refrain from presenting responsible officers or officers in charge in local municipalities or government agencies with money and goods or otherwise benefiting them in an effort to win competitive superiority.

1.6 **Respecting Intellectual Property Rights**

To refrain from infringing on the intellectual property rights owned by competitors, such as their brands and patents.

VI. 競争会社

1. 法的責任
1.1 各国の反トラスト法又は競争法,関連法令等の遵守

競争会社との間では,各国の反トラスト法又は競争法を遵守し,公正に,そして合法的に競争する.

1.2 私的独占の禁止
競争会社の企業活動を不当に妨害したり,ボイコット等市場からの追い出しを図るような私的独占は行わない.

1.3 不当な取引制限の禁止
同業他社及び業界団体との間で共同して価格の決定や維持又は値上げ,生産・販売数量などの協定や受注予定者を決定する不当な取引制限にあたるカルテルや談合は行わない.

1.4 不公正な取引方法の禁止
競争会社のビジネスに対して不当廉売や競争者に対する取引妨害などの不公正な取引方法は行わない.

1.5 公務員への贈賄の禁止
競争上の優位を得るために,自治体や官公庁の担当者や責任者に金品を贈ったり,便益を与えるような行為は行わない.

1.6 知的財産権の尊重
競争会社のブランドや特許などの知的財産権を侵害しない.

1.7 Ban on Giving Bribes to Customers' Employees

To refrain from presenting responsible persons or persons in charge in customers' companies with money and goods beyond the boundaries of socially acceptable limits in an effort to win competitive superiority.

1.8 Ban on Unfair Competition

To abide by the Unfair Competition Prevention Law in collecting market information, such as that on competitors' new technologies, new products and commercial information including consumers, without using illegal means, such as bribery and spying.

2. Economic Responsibility

2.1 Contributing to a Free Economic Society

To compete with other firms in the same line of business in developing new technologies and products to contribute to the growth of the industry and a free economic society.

2.2 Forging Favorable Partnership

To forge relationships of mutual benefit with competitors, out of the notion that competitors could turn into suppliers, customers or partners or otherwise come to have multiphase trade relations.

3. Ethical Commitment

3.1 Relationships with Competitors

To refrain from using expressions or conducting acts that are aimed at detracting specific competitors and aim to achieve the growth of the industry as a whole through self-restrained competition with competitors.

3.2 Normalizing Access to Information

To collect market information, such as that on competitors' new tech-

1.7　取引先企業の従業員への贈賄の禁止

競争上の優位を得るために，企業の担当者や責任者に社会通念を越えた金品を贈ったり，便益を与えるような行為は行わない．

1.8　不正競争の防止

競争会社の新技術や新製品，消費者などの営業情報の入手にあたっては，不正競争防止法を遵守し，情報の金銭による買収やスパイ的行為など，その他違法な手段は用いない．

2.　経済的責任
2.1　自由経済社会への寄与

同業他社との間で新技術や新製品の開発に切磋琢磨し，業界や自由経済社会の発展に寄与する．

2.2　良好なパートナーシップの醸成

競争会社が取引先になったり，パートナーになったり多面的な取引関係をもつことがあり得ることを認識して両者にとってプラスとなるような関係を構築する．

3.　倫理的責任
3.1　競争会社との関係

特定の競争会社を誹謗・中傷する表現や行為を慎み，競争会社との節度ある競争を通して業界全体の発展を目指す．

3.2　情報入手の適正化

競争会社の新技術や新製品，消費者などの営業情報は誠実で公正な方法で入

nologies, new products and consumers, in a sincere and faith method.

3.3 Dealing with Trade Associations

To refrain from attending meetings or parties held by other firms in the same line of business or by trade associations when such meetings or parties are likely to cause misunderstanding.

3.4 Reforming Trade Practices

To cooperate as an active member of a trade organization in terminating antisocial or unethical acts, such as traditional inappropriate trade practices (such as collusive biddings at the initiative of governmental agencies).

3.5 Transparent Relations with Politicians

To build sound and normal relations with politicians and governmental agency personnel to benefit the industry as a whole.

3.6 Eliminating Antisocial Groups and Organizations

To collaborate as a member of the industry in eliminating antisocial groups or organizations.

4. Community Commitment

4.1 Supporting the Socially Vulnerable

To provide positive assistance to the socially vulnerable, developing countries and so forth as a member of a trade association by working in conjunction with the administration and governmental agencies concerned.

4.2 Mutual Aid in Times of Natural Disasters

To provide goods, such as products and services, for a certain period of time on behalf of competitors when the competitors become unable to make them available in times of natural disasters.

手する．

3.3 適正な業界団体との対応
同業他社や業界団体の付き合いにおいて誤解を受ける会合や飲食会には出席しない．

3.4 商習慣の改革
業界団体の一員として相互に協力し，従来の商慣習（例えば官製談合など）のような反社会的，非倫理的行為を積極的に撲滅するよう働きかける．

3.5 政治家との透明な関係
業界全体の利益となるように，政治家や官公庁の職員とは健全かつ正常な関係を構築する．

3.6 反社会的勢力・団体の排除
業界団体の一員として相互に協力し，反社会的勢力・団体の排除に取り組む．

4. 社会貢献的責任

4.1 社会的弱者等への支援
社会的弱者，途上国等への支援は，行政，関係政府と連携し業界団体として積極的に行う．

4.2 災害時の相互扶助
災害時，競争会社が製品やサービスなどの財の提供を継続し得ない状況になった場合，一定期間，競争会社に代わりこれらの提供を行う．

4.3 Partnering with NPOs/NGOs

To take active part in social contribution and conservative activities of global environment by partnering with NPOs/NGOs as a member of a trade association.

4.4 Taking Active Part in Social Contribution Activities as a Good Corporate Citizen

To search for social contribution activities of highly common interest together with competitors (trade association) in fields closely related to the industry and actively conduct social contribution and conservative activities of global environment, including joint human or monetary aid to volunteer groups and NPOs/NGOs.

4.5 Disclosing the Status of Social Contribution Activities

To document and actively publicize approaches to social contribution and conservative activities of global environment in Social and Environment Reports, CSR Reports, and Sustainability Reports as a member of a trade association, including competitors.

4.6 Supporting the Resolution of Social Issues

To try to resolve the social issues arising at the point of contact between the industry, including competitors, and its stakeholders by offering financial assistance and sector-specific human resources, taking advantage of the power of networking and so forth by working in conjunction with the government, NPOs/NGOs, competitors (trade association) and others.

4.3 NPO/NGO との連携

業界団体として NPO/NGO と協力して，地球環境問題や社会貢献活動に積極的に取り組む．

4.4 "良き企業市民"として積極的に社会貢献活動への参画

産業とかかわりの深い分野において，競争会社（業界団体）とともに公益性の高い社会貢献活動を模索し，共同で寄付やボランティア組織，NPO/NGO への人的支援などを含め，積極的に社会貢献，地球環境保全活動を実施する．

4.5 社会貢献活動状況の開示

競争会社を含む業界団体として，社会貢献，地球環境保全活動などへの取組みを"社会・環境報告書"，"CSR 報告書"，"持続可能性報告書"など作成し，相互に積極的に開示する．

4.6 社会的課題への支援

競争会社を含む業界とそのステークホルダーとの接点において発生している社会的課題に対し，政府，NPO/NGO，競争会社（業界団体）などと連携し，資金提供，各セクターの人的資源，ネットワークなどを活用して，社会的課題の解決を図る．

VII. Mass Media

1. Legal Responsibility

1.1 Disclosing Facts

To disclose all factual information to mass media reporters as it is, except for trade secrets and personal information in compliance with the relevant laws and regulations, without making false statements and misleading the reporters.

1.2 Ban on Manipulating Information Illicitly

To refrain from manipulating information to disclose to mass media when it could led to a rigging of stock prices.

1.3 Making Global Responses

To allow for concurrent releases to domestic and foreign media by allowing for their time differences when such releases could have a global impact and disclose information in the best manner to meet the governing foreign codes or laws.

1.4 Non-infringement on Intellectual Property Rights

To refrain from disclosing information to mass media or manipulating mass media when such disclosure or manipulation could infringe on privacy, defamation, infringe on someone's right of portrait, and otherwise infringe on intellectual property rights, such as copyrights.

2. Economic Responsibility

2.1 Disclosing Sensitive Information

To respond to mass media reporters seeking socially significant information, including financial and accounting information, in a sincere attitude without decimations and without turning down the interviews, and hold press conferences in the presence of company leaders

VII. マスメディア

1. 法的責任
1.1 事実の開示
　マスメディアの取材に対しては，企業機密や個人情報に関することを除き，事実をありのままに開示し，虚偽の発言やミスリードを行わず法令を遵守する．

1.2 違法な情報操作の禁止
　マスメディアに対して株価操作につながる可能性をもつ情報操作は行わない．

1.3 グローバルな対応
　グローバルな影響をもつ情報の開示では，時差を勘案した内外メディアへの同時発表なども考慮するとともに，諸外国の規範・法令に対応した最善の情報開示を行う．

1.4 知的財産権の不侵害
　プライバシーの侵害，名誉毀損，肖像権の侵害，著作権などの知的財産権の侵害につながる，マスメディアへの情報開示やマスメデイア操作を行わない．

2. 経済的責任
2.1 重要情報の開示
　財務・会計情報を含む社会的に重要な情報についてのマスメディアの取材に対しては，差別することなく真摯(しんし)に対応し，取材拒否をしないとともに経営トップないし関係者の出席のもと記者発表を行うなどマスメディアに適時適切に情報を開示する．

or others concerned to disclose relevant information to the mass media in a proper and timely manner.

2.2 Public Hearing

To collect unprocessed opinions, views and advise broadly from the public through mass media and feed them back to the internal organization.

2.3 Maintaining a Scheme of Crisis Communication

To get the concept of the crisis communication down through to the bottom of the corporate organization as part of crisis management to maintain a scheme of information transmission and run a simulation to handle emergencies as they arise.

2.4 Disclosing Information on the Internet

To disclose economically significant information positively at a web site on the Internet.

2.5 Responding to False Information and Rumors

To ask mass media to correct false articles or coverages to resolve public misunderstanding when such articles are of great economic significance, and to disclose facts about rumors of great economic significance with the cooperation of mass media and post facts at a web site on the Internet, instead of leaving rumors on the loose.

3. Ethical Commitment

3.1 Responding Properly in Times of Scandals

To find facts about scandals, such as revealed by whistle blowers, questioned by mass media and respond to them promptly.

To install countermeasure headquarters in the company in case of significant problem and make uniform views available as in a position paper, disclosing the information on such occasions as emergency

2.2 広聴

マスメディアを介した社会の意見・アドバイスなど生の声を広く収集し，内部にフィードバックする．

2.3 クライシス・コミュニケーション体制の整備

危機管理の一環として，クライシス・コミュニケーション意識の醸成をはかり，緊急時の情報伝達ルートの整備と対応シミュレーションを実施する．

2.4 インターネットによる情報開示

自社のホームページなどのインターネットを通じて，経済的に重要な情報を積極的に開示する．

2.5 誤報や風評への対応

マスメディアを通じ経済的に大きな影響がある，誤った記事・報道が提供されている場合，その訂正をマスメディアに求め，社会の誤解を解く努力をする．また，経済的に大きな影響がある風評に対しても，マスメディアの協力を得て事実を開示するとともに，自社のホームページなどのインターネットを介して，風評が一人歩きしないように努める．

3. 倫理的責任
3.1 不祥事発生時の適切な対応

内部告発など，マスメディアからの不祥事の問い合わせには，事実を確認し，迅速に回答する．また，状況に応じて，社内に対策本部を設置し，ポジションペーパーなどで統一見解を用意し，緊急記者会見等でマスメディアに情報を開示する．新たな不祥事が発生したときには，国民感情なども配慮した発言や対応を行う．

press conferences; to release statements come up with responses to allow for national sentiments when new scandals arise.

3.2 Disclosing Negative Information

To disclose even negative information to mass media without delay when it is likely to exert an adverse effect, such as a defective product or accident, on the society, and try to post relevant information at a web site on the Internet as needed, in addition to putting an announcement advertisement such as one calling for a recall.

3.3 Responding in Good Faith

To refrain from releasing malicious information that detracts competitors to mass media and from interfering with interviews from mass media and coverages.

3.4 Responding to Serious Events

To post information at a web site on the Internet positively to provide an account of any defective product or event occurring to threaten a serious impact on the social life, such as one risking human lives or health, thereby facilitating two-way communication.

4. Community Commitment

4.1 Disclosing the Status of Social Contribution and Conservative Activities of Global Environment

To commit the management philosophy or code of conduct relating to social contribution and conservative activities of global environment to mass media and positively disclose information about ongoing approaches to implementing these activities.

4.2 Releasing Information about Social Contribution and Conservative Activities of Global Environment

To positively disclose information and know-how that are beneficial to

3.2 マイナス情報の開示

欠陥製品や事故など社会に悪影響を及ぼす可能性のある場合は，マイナス情報であっても遅滞なくマスメディアに開示する．さらに，必要があるときは，例えばリコールなどの告知広告を実施するとともに，自社のホームページなどのインターネットを通じた情報開示に努める．

3.3 誠実な対応

競合企業を誹謗・中傷するなど悪意に満ちた情報提供を，マスメディアに対して行わない．また，マスメディアの取材や記事掲載などに対して妨害工作をしない．

3.4 重大事象への対応

欠陥製品や人命・健康など社会生活に重大な影響を及ぼす事象が発生した場合は，マスメディアに対し積極的に情報を提供するとともに，自社のホームページなどのインターネットを介してツーウェイのコミュニケーションが円滑に進むよう努力する．

4. 社会貢献的責任

4.1 社会貢献，地球環境保全活動状況の開示

社会貢献，地球環境保全活動に関する経営理念や行動基準をマスメディアにコミットするとともに，社会貢献活動，地球環境保全活動への取組みに関する情報を積極的に開示する．

4.2 社会貢献，地球環境保全活動情報の提供

社会貢献，地球環境保全活動に取り組む NPO などに有益な情報・ノウハウ

NPOs engaged in social contribution and conservative activities of global environment through mass media and web site on the Internet, thereby contributing to the growth of the society as a good corporate citizen.

4.3 Taking Part in Social Contribution and Conservative Activities of Global Environment

To take active part in the social contribution campaigns sponsored by mass media and release information, jointly with mass media, to stir public interests in issues, such as local and global environments, and human rights.

をマスメディアやインターネットを通じて積極的に開示し，良き企業市民として社会の発展に寄与する．

4.3 社会貢献，地球環境保全活動への参画

マスメディアが主宰する社会貢献キャンペーンに積極的に参加するとともに，地域，地球環境，人権問題などへの社会的関心を啓発する発信をマスメディアと共同で行う．

VIII. Administration

1. **Legal Responsibility**

1.1 **Maintaining Safety and Respecting Human Rights in Administrative Districts**

To comply with all governing laws and regulations relating to disaster prevention, architecture, security and traffic safety, and labor safety and health in conducting corporate activities to maintain safety in administrative districts and also respect human rights in compliance with laws and regulations of human rights.

1.2 **Complying with Environmental Standards, Implementing Maintenance Measures, and Disclosing Information**

To put into action various measures aimed at maintaining human health and preserving the living environment in compliance with the environmental standards set by the nation and communities, and report to the administration the volumes of emissions of the chemical substances, controlled as being harmful to human health, and publicize them in an appropriate manner.

1.3 **Disposing of Waste Properly and Using Cyclically Reusable Resources**

To control and dispose of the waste arising from the implementation of corporate activities properly in accordance with prescribed laws and standards, and put cyclically reusable resources arising from the implementation of corporate activities to reuse or recycle them in accordance with prescribed standards.

1.4 **Abiding by Trade Codes and Ban on Bribing Civil Servants**

To require compliance with relevant laws and regulations, including the Antimonopoly law, to conduct fair trade practices in selling prod-

VIII. 行政

1. 法的責任

1.1 行政区域内の安全確保と人権尊重

　企業活動にあたっては，防災・建築に関する規制法令，治安・交通安全及び労働・安全衛生に関する法令等を遵守し，行政区域内の安全確保を図ると同時に，人権に関する法令等を遵守して人権尊重を実現する．

1.2 環境基準の遵守と保全対策の実施並びにその情報公開

　人の健康の維持及び生活環境の保全を図るため，国及び地域が定めた環境基準を遵守し，環境保全のための各種対策を実施する．また，有害で規制対象となる化学物質についてはその排出量を行政に報告し，適切に公表する．

1.3 廃棄物の適正処理と循環資源の利用

　企業活動において発生した廃棄物については，関係する法令・基準に従って適正に管理・処理する．また，企業活動中に利用・発生する循環資源については定められた基準に従って再生利用又は再資源化する．

1.4 商取引関連法規の遵守と公務員への贈賄等の禁止

　製品やサービスの販売に際しては独禁法をはじめとした商取引関連法規を遵守して，公正な商取引を行う．特に行政に対しては公明正大な商取引を心がけ

ucts and services, particularly to the administration, and refrain from colluding with or bribing civil servants.

2. Economic Responsibility

2.1 Sound Corporate Activities and Responsibility for Employment

To execute required development, procurement, production, and sales activities in an appropriate and sound manner to fulfill the responsibility for employment and business execution while making human and physical investment of a size matched to the scale of business.

2.2 Due Tax Obligation

To pay corporate taxes and other duly payable taxes to fulfill the responsibility for taxation to the national and municipal governments while earning fair profits through sound corporate activities and fair accounting and closing procedures.

3. Ethical Commitment

3.1 Positive Cooperation in Administrative Activities

To provide positive support and cooperation in the administrative guidance and approaches of the administration, as for environmental standards, and safety and health, to bolter environmental preservation and social security.

3.2 Relations with the Administration

To take active part and cooperate in the process of formulating administrative policies, plans and standards to represent public view while maintaining a stance of equality with the administration.

3.3 Disclosing Information, and Accountability

To actively disclose the corporate information to the administration

るとともに公務員との間で癒着や贈収賄を発生させない．

2. 経済的責任
2.1 健全な企業活動と雇用責任

　事業規模に見合った適切な人的・物的投資を行いつつ，事業遂行に必要な開発・調達・生産・販売活動を適切かつ健全に遂行して雇用責任・事業遂行責任を果たす．

2.2 適正な納税責任
　健全な企業活動と適正な決算・会計処理によって適正な利益を確保し，法人税をはじめとした諸税を適正に支払い，国と地方の行政に対する納税責任を全うする．

3. 倫理的責任
3.1 行政の活動に対する積極的な協力
　環境保全，社会安全の確保をより一層図るため，行政が取り組む環境基準や安全・衛生等に関する行政指導，取組みに対して積極的に支援，協力する．

3.2 行政との関係
　行政との関係については対等な立場を堅持するとともに，行政政策・計画や基準策定に対し，民意の反映を目指して，前向きに参画・協力する．

3.3 情報開示と説明責任
　行政・社会に対して企業情報を積極的に開示し，説明責任を適切に果たして，

and communities and fulfill the obligation for accountability, thereby maintaining the transparency of corporate activities.

3.4 Confronting Antisocial Groups and Organizations

To declare a firm resolutions in and outside the company to decisively eliminate antisocial groups or organizations that threaten the order and security of the civil society and tackle to eliminate them by working in conjunction with trade associations and local enterprises and collaborating with the police to counter threats.

3.5 Respecting National and Regional Cultures and Customs

To conduct corporate activities in full respect of the national and regional cultures and customs with the social and ethical characteristics in the communities.

4. Community Commitment

4.1 Contributing to and Supporting Social Contribution Activities

To provide positive support and contribution to the welfare, volunteer, cultural, artistic and sport activities conducted by the administration taking advantage of the company's own managerial resources.

4.2 Cooperation in and Support to Conservative Activities of Global Environment

To provide positive support and contribution to conservative activities of global environment conducted at the administration's initiative as a good corporate citizen.

4.3 Implementing Donation Activities

To donate corresponding amounts of money, if necessary, to the social contribution and conservative activities of global environment deployed by the administration and provide positive support and contribution to the associated donation activities.

事業運営の透明性を確保する．

3.4 反社会的勢力・団体との対決姿勢
　市民社会の秩序や安全に脅威を与える反社会的勢力・団体に対しては断固として排除する姿勢を明確に社内外に宣言する．業界団体，地域企業及び行政と連携して排除に取り組むとともに，威嚇(いかく)に対しては，警察等と連携するなどして毅然と対抗する．

3.5 国・地域の文化・慣習の尊重
　当地における社会性や倫理性を考慮し，国・地域の文化・慣習を十分に尊重した企業活動を行う．

4. 社会貢献的責任
4.1 社会貢献活動への協力，支援
　行政が取り組む福祉・ボランティア活動や芸術・文化・体育活動等を自社の経営資源を生かしながら積極的に支援，貢献する．

4.2 地球環境保全活動への協力，支援

　良き企業市民として，行政が主体的に取り組む地球環境保全活動に対して積極的に支援，貢献する．

4.3 寄付活動の実施
　行政が関与する社会貢献活動や，地球環境保全活動に対し，必要に応じて応分の寄付を行うとともに，関連する寄付活動に対しても積極的に協力，支援する．

IX. NPOs/NGOs

1. Legal Responsibility

1.1 Complying with International Rules and Relevant Laws and Regulations

To comply with international rules and the laws and regulations in effect in a target region to establish and maintain fair relations with NPOs and NGOs.

1.2 Ban on Unfair Responses

To treat NPOs and NGOs in a fair, impartial and sincere attitude in respect of their action philosophy and guidelines and refrain from infringing on any of their unique activities.

1.3 Ban on Abuse of Dominant Bargaining Positions

To maintain mutually fair relations of information disclosure, cooperation and so forth with NPOs and NGOs, and refrain from giving discriminative treatment to them or abusing dominant bargaining positions based on their sizes and activities, and detracting specific NPOs and NGOs.

1.4 Ban on Reciprocating Trade

To maintain co-existence and co-prosperity with NPOs and NGOs and refrain from conducting reciprocating trade in violation of fair market rules.

1.5 Protecting Personal Information

To place and safeguard under strict management such personal information that is collected in the course of linkage and collaborative activities with NPOs and NGOs to prevent its leakage and inappropriateuse.

IX. NPO/NGO

1. 法的責任
1.1 国際ルールと関連法令の遵守

NPO/NGO と適正な関係を確立・維持するため，国際ルール及び当該地域の法令を遵守する．

1.2 不公正な対応の禁止
NPO/NGO の活動理念・方針を尊重し，公正・公平で誠実な態度で接するとともに，いかなる NPO/NGO 独自の活動も侵害しない．

1.3 優越的地位の濫用の禁止
企業と NPO/NGO が相互に適切な情報公開，協力など公正な関係を維持する．NPO/NGO の規模・活動内容による差別的な取扱いや優越的地位の濫用，特定の NPO/NGO への誹謗・中傷を行わない．

1.4 互恵取引の禁止
企業と NPO/NGO が相互の共存共栄を維持するとともに，公正な市場ルールに反するような互恵取引を行わない．

1.5 個人情報の保護
NPO/NGO との連携・協働活動によって得られた個人情報については，情報漏洩や不正な利用等がないように厳重に管理する．

2. Economic Responsibility

2.1 Defining Managerial Resource Information

To define corporate principles, guidelines and target products in conducting linkage and collaborative activities with NPOs and NGOs and quantify the range or kinds of managerial resources that can be made available to them, publicizing such information as needed.

2.2 Conducting Linkage and Collaborative Activities

To promote the implementation of linkage and collaborative activities with NPOs and NGOs in a fair manner, as by defining corporate principles, guidelines and target products and make required managerial resources available to them to bolster their economic structure.

2.3 Dispatching Employees

To expressly advice that the employees are to be transferred to a cooperating organization as part of routine workflow with forming a regulation.

2.4 Loaning and Lending Assets

To loan and lend tangible assets, such as fixture and facilities, in one's possession to NPOs and NGOs in an appropriate fashion adhering to relevant laws and regulations. Particularly, relevant business documents need to be sorted in order and studied before tangible assets relating to technological patent rights and intellectual property rights can be made available to NPOs and NGOs.

3. Ethical Commitment

3.1 Linkage and Collaboration

To prioritize those products that can contribute to the growth of a sound civil society in conducting linkage and collaborative activities with NPOs and NGOs and refrain from executing those projects that

2. 経済的責任

2.1 経営資源情報の確定

NPO/NGOとの連携・協働活動を行うにあたっては，企業としての理念・方針を確立するとともに，提供可能な経営資源の範囲又は内容を可能な限り数量化し，必要な場合にその情報を公表する．

2.2 連携・協働活動の実施

連携・協働活動の相手先及び活動内容を選定する場合には，企業の理念・方針及び成果目標を明示するなど公正な手段によって推進し，所定の経営資源の供与を行い，NPO/NGOの経済基盤の強化を支援する．

2.3 従業員の派遣

従業員を協働する組織に派遣する場合には，規程類の整備を行って業務の一環として実施することを従業員に明示して実施する．

2.4 資産の貸与，供与

企業が保有する備品，施設など有形資産を提供する場合には，関係法令に従い適切な方法で実施する．特に技術などの特許権，知的財産権にかかわる無形資産の提供を行う場合は，事前に権利関係を整理・検討した上で実施する．

3. 倫理的責任

3.1 連携・協働

NPO/NGOとの連携・協働においては，健全な市民社会の発展に資する成果を優先し，経済的利益追求だけを重視するプロジェクトは行わない．

pursue economic profits only.

3.2 Criteria for Selecting Collaborative Projects

To select collaborative projects with the own corporate guidelines and principles being weighed against the sociality, ethics, effectiveness and other characteristics of NPOs and NGOs.

3.3 Disclosing Information

To disclose information about the recipient organizations to which employees have been assigned, donations given, and facilities made available, the kinds of such offerings, and the resultant output to the extent possible.

3.4 Responding to Bribery, Excessive Gifting and Entertainment

To refrain from soliciting private profits (such as money, goods and services) and forcing bribery in dealing with NPOs and NGOs, and also refrain from excessive gifting and entertainment.

3.5 Terminating Relations with Antisocial Groups and Organizations

To break up relations with antisocial groups or organizations decisively, regardless of whether such relations convey ordinary urges or requests or not.

4. Community Commitment

4.1 Supporting NPOs/NGOs

To provide a scheme of organizational administration and management techniques that would enable NPOs and NGOs to effectively function in all areas of social activity for the purpose of achieving sound social growth.

4.2 Making Facilities and Equipment Accessible

To make the facilities and equipment held by the company accessible

3.2 協働関係先の選択基準

企業は NPO/NGO と連携・協働するプロジェクトについては，自社の理念・方針と NPO/NGO 活動の社会性，倫理性，効果性などに照らし合わせて選択する．

3.3 情報公開

人員派遣や寄付，貸与，供与など実施した先の組織及び内容だけでなく，可能な限りその成果情報も公表する．

3.4 賄賂，過度な贈答・接待への対応

NPO/NGO との関係では，私的な利益，便益（金銭，物品，サービスなど），賄賂を強制しない．また，相互に社会常識に反するような，過度な贈答・接待を行わない．

3.5 反社会的勢力・団体との関係根絶

反社会的勢力・団体に対しては，通常の要請・要望であっても関係を絶ち，断固として対決する．

4. 社会貢献的責任

4.1 NPO/NGO 組織への支援

健全な社会の発展のためには，あらゆる社会活動領域において NPO/NGO 組織が効果的に機能していくような組織運営・経営手法を提供する．

4.2 施設，設備等の開放

企業が保有する各種施設，設備等を NPO/NGO や一般市民に開放し，地域

to NPOs and NGOs pursuing social welfare and environmental conservation activities to contribute to sound growth of the local communities.

4.3 Supporting Social Contribution and Conservative Activities of Global Environment

To provide positive assistance to NPOs and NGOs pursuing to protect and promote cultures and arts, and promoting social welfare and conservative activities of global environment to contribute to the sound growth of the local communities.

4.4 Taking Part in Social Contribution and Conservative Activities of Global Environment

To take active part in the work of NPOs and NGOs pursuing social contribution and conservative activities of global environment to contribute to the sustainable growth of both the company and local communities.

社会へ貢献するとともに良好なコミュニケーションの構築を図る．

4.3 社会貢献・地球環境活動の支援

　文化，芸術などの保護，振興や社会福祉，地球環境保全活動等を進めるNPO/NGOを積極的に支援し，地域社会の健全な発展にも寄与する．

4.4 社会貢献・地球環境活動への参画

　社会貢献・地球環境保全活動を推進するNPO/NGOの活動に積極的に参画し，企業が目指す企業と社会の持続可能な発展に貢献する．

X. International Community

1. Legal Responsibility

1.1 Complying with International Rules, and Japanese and Local Laws

To abide by the international rules and codes, such as ISO, as a member of the international community and comply with the laws and regulations in effect in the country of operation, conducting fair corporate activities with unfair and partial acts being removed.

1.2 Respecting Human Rights

To respect human rights, which are to human beings. Whenever a case of a violation of human rights is known to the company, it shall take corrective action immediately, regardless of the nationality, race, gender, sexual orientation, age, origin, academic career, personal connections, disabilities, religion and other characteristics of the affected.

1.3 Ban on Child Labor and Forced Labor

To ban the labor of children and undue forced labor of employees against their will. In addition, the labor laws and regulations in effect in the country of operation shall apply.

1.4 Ban on Discrimination of Employees at Recruitment, Employment, Promotion, Labor Conditions, Wages and Training

To refrain from discriminating employees in terms of recruitment, employment, promotion, labor conditions, wages and training for reasons of their nationality, race, gender, sexual orientation, age, origin, academic career, personal connections, disabilities, religion and other characteristics.

1.5 Maintaining and Promoting Safety and Health

To endeavor to protect the safety and health of the residents in the

X. 国際社会

1. 法的責任
1.1 国際ルールや日本国及び現地の法令の遵守

　国際社会の一員として国際ルールやISOなどの各種規格を守るとともに，事業を行う国の法令を遵守し，不正・不当な行動を排除し適正な企業活動を行う．

1.2 人権の尊重
　人権は，人間が人間として固有の権利であり，これを尊重する．企業は，人権が侵される行為などを知り得たときは，直ちに是正する処置を行う．これは，国籍，人種，性別，性的指向性，年齢，出身，学歴，縁戚関係，障害，宗教等によって変わるべきものではない．

1.3 強制労働と児童労働の禁止
　強制労働及び児童労働は理由のいかんを問わずこれを禁止する．その他，事業を行う国での労働関係法令を遵守する．

1.4 求人，雇用，昇進，労働条件，賃金，研修での差別の禁止

　国籍，人種，性別，性的指向性，年齢，出身，学歴，縁戚関係，障害，宗教等で従業員の雇用，昇進，労働条件，賃金については差別を行わない．

1.5 安全と健康の維持・増進
　企業活動については，従業員だけでなく事業を行う地域の住民の安全及び健

region of operation, as well as employees engaged in the corporate activities, and fulfill all the obligations for environmental conservation, safe and health that apply in the country and region of operation.

1.6 Forming an Acceptable Landscape

To create a pleasant, wealthy living environment and build an artistic, elegant society in compliance with the relevant laws and regulations in the country and region of operation that are committed to forming an acceptable landscape, thereby aiming to form an individualistic and vital local community.

1.7 Ban on Corruption

To refrain from conducting any act of bribery or profit sharing with foreign civil servants, such as officers for foreign governments or municipalities, in international trade.

1.8 Ban on Abuse of Dominant Bargaining Positions

To refrain from giving discriminative treatment or abusing dominant bargaining positions based on economy size and international position.

1.9 Elimination of Inappropriate Payment Methods

To refrain from receiving funds derived from criminal acts or accepting any method of payment that could assist in money laundering.

2. Economic Responsibility

2.1 Proper Tax Obligation

To duly fulfill the obligation for payment that is defined in the country and region of operation and act as a good corporate citizen.

2.2 Fair Wage Payment

To pay employees wages in an amount matched to the amount of

康に留意し，これらの保護に努める．また，事業を行うすべての地域・国で定められた，環境及び安全衛生上の義務をすべて果たす．

1.6 良好な景観の形成
　事業を行う国及び地域が実施する良好な景観の形成にかかわる法令・規制を遵守し，潤いある豊かな生活環境の創造及び芸術的で情緒ある社会の実現を図るとともに，ひいては個性的で活力のある地域社会の実現を目指す．

1.7 国際間腐敗防止
　国際取引において，外国政府・地方公共団体の役職員など，外国公務員等に対し贈賄行為や利益供与の行為は行わない．

1.8 優越的地位の濫用の禁止
　経済や国際的地位などの国家的優位性を利用した不当な差別的取扱いなど優越的地位の濫用を行わない．

1.9 不適切な支払方法への無関与
　犯罪行為から得た資金の受領や，不正な資金洗浄（マネーロンダリング）への関与は行わない．

2. 経済的責任
2.1 納税の義務
　事業を行うすべての地域・国家にて定められた納税義務は適切に遂行し，良き企業市民として行動しなければならない．
2.2 妥当な賃金支給
　賃金に対しては，労働力に見合った妥当な対価を，事業を行う地域・国家の

labor provided, in full consideration of the labor practices in the region and country of operation.

2.3 Fair and Impartial Personnel Evaluation

To give personnel ratings to employees in a fair and impartial manner without discrimination for reasons of their nationality, race, sex, sexual preference, age, origin, academic career, personal connections, disabilities and other characteristics.

2.4 Fair Welfare Program and Measures

To implement an equivalent of the welfare program and measures in effect in the parent country with local characteristics reflected in it.

2.5 Supporting Employee Education and Ability Development

To provide training for knowledge and skill required for jobs by OJT (On the Job Training) and OFF-JT (Off the Job Training), or provide positive assistance to employees who need to acquire the elementary and prerequisite knowledge and skill for jobs.

2.6 Safe and Clean Workplace

To keep the workplace safe and clean at all times and be ready to improve on the workshop immediately without hesitation if it is felt possibly hazardous to employees or harmful to health.

2.7 Disclosing Corporate Information

To disclose all corporate information in all regions and countries without omission, regardless of whether the information is of advantageous nature or not.

2.8 Fair Corporate Activities

To pay due taxes by the rule through fair corporate activities, thereby contributing to the growth of the local economy and community.

2.9 Boosting the Level of Technology

To endeavor to boost the level of technology so as to make good prod-

労働慣習を十分考慮して支給する．

2.3　公平かつ公正な人事評価
人事評価については，国籍，人種，性別，性的指向性，年齢，出身，学歴，縁戚関係，障害，宗教等で差別することなく，公平かつ公正な人事評価を行う．

2.4　妥当な福利厚生制度・施策
福利厚生制度及び施策については現地の状況を踏まえ，本国の制度及び施策と同水準で行う．

2.5　従業員教育，能力向上の支援
業務に関する従業員の知識及び技術に関する教育は，OJT（On the Job Training：職場内訓練）及びOFF-JT（Off the Job Training：職場外訓練）にて行わなければならない．また，業務以前の基礎学力が不足している場合には能力向上のための支援も積極的に行う．

2.6　安全かつ清潔な職場環境
職場は，常に安全かつ清潔な環境を保たなければならない．もし職場が従業員に対して危険である，又は健康に有害であると感ずる場合には躊躇（ちゅうちょ）なく速やかにその改善に努める．

2.7　企業情報の公開
企業は，自社に有利，不利に関係なくあらゆる情報をすべての地域・国家に対して怠りなく，公開しなければならない．

2.8　適正な企業活動
適正な企業活動を通して，適正な税金をルールどおり納める．これらを通じ現地の経済及び社会の発展に寄与する．

2.9　技術水準の向上
事業を行う地域・国家と協調して，良い製品やサービスが提供できるような

ucts and services available by working in conjunction with the region and country of operation.

2.10 Providing Rational and Economic Values

To provide consumers with rational and economic values tailored to their needs.

3. Ethical Commitment

3.1 Establishing a Compliance Program

To have a compliance program built in position to make a scandal-free organization and get all the employees educated and trained in the international rules, the laws and regulations in effect in the country of operation and other rules to be observed.

3.2 Conducting Fair and Impartial Corporate Activities as a Good Corporate Citizen

To direct the company to carry out corporate activities as a good corporate citizen in a fair, impartial manner in all the countries and regions of operation.

3.3 Sincere Response and Grievance Procedures

To respond to various consumer queries, complaints or claims in good faith and promptly, in a fair and impartial manner, regardless of where the consumers live.

3.4 Responding Crisis Management

To institute, for example, a compliance committee, CSR department or any other specialized division dedicated to crisis management, to entertain complaints received from inside and outside the company and to prevent business scandals or handle scandals if they occur.

3.5 Respecting Local Cultures and Customs

To conduct corporate activities in full respect of the local cultures, his-

技術水準の向上に努める．

2.10 合理的で経済的な価値の提供
世界の消費者のニーズを把握し，合理的で経済的な価値を提供する．

3. 倫理的責任
3.1 コンプライアンス体制の確立
不祥事を起こさない組織をつくるために，コンプライアンス体制を整えるとともに，全従業員に国際ルール，事業を行う国の法令，守るべき規則などの教育，研修を行う．

3.2 良き企業市民としての公平かつ公正な企業活動

企業はすべての企業活動として，関係のあるすべての地域・国家においても，良き企業市民として公平かつ公正であり誠実な企業活動を行う．

3.3 誠実な対応・苦情処理
消費者等からの様々な問い合わせや不平・不満などの申し出，苦情・要望などには誠実かつ迅速に対応する．これは，消費者の地域・国家にかかわらず，公平及び公正に行われるべきである．

3.4 危機管理への対応
企業内外からの苦情の対応や企業内の不祥事などを未然に防ぐため，又は万一不祥事が発生した場合の対応のために，例えばコンプライアンス委員会やCSR部などの専門の部署を設け，危機管理に努める．

3.5 現地の文化・慣習の尊重
現地の文化，歴史，慣習，景観を理解した上で，これらを尊重し，十分配慮

tories, customs, and landscapes.

3.6 Responding to Diversity

To pay full respect to all people without prejudice or discrimination for reasons of their nationality, race, gender, sexual orientation, age, origin, academic career, personal connections, disabilities and other characteristics discrimination by which is banned by law.

3.7 Heeding Conservation of Global Environment

To promote global corporate activities to deliver fully eco-friendly products and services.

3.8 Confronting Antisocial Groups and Organizations

To terminate dealings with antisocial groups and organizations such as international terrorists plotting destructive acts or with countries seeking to manufacture internationally banned weapons of mass-destruction.

4. Community Commitment

4.1 Protecting Natural Environments and Global Resources

To endeavor to protect and preserve intact the global, as well as local, natural environments and resources positively.

4.2 Supporting Social Contribution Activities and Volunteerism

To take active part in social contribution activities and volunteerism in the country where the company operates as a global enterprise, and support participation of employees in these activities, with aids and volunteerism being concentrated on economically disadvantageous countries and regions.

4.3 Taking Active Part in Local Community Activities

To take active part in local community events as a member of the local community in the country of operation and as a good corporate

した経営活動を行う．

3.6 多様性への対応

国籍，人種，性別，性的指向性，年齢，出身，学歴，縁戚関係，障害，その他法令により差別を禁じられている性質によって，偏見や差別を行うことなく，いかなる人に対しても敬意を払わなければならない．

3.7 地球環境保全への配慮

地球環境保全を十分配慮した製品やサービスの提供に努め，グローバルな企業活動を推進する．

3.8 反社会的勢力・団体及び国家との対決

破壊的行為を遂行する国際的テロリストなどの反社会的勢力・団体や国際的に禁止されている大量破壊兵器の製造を企てている国家との取引は根絶する．

4. 社会貢献的責任

4.1 自然環境・地球資源の保護

現地の自然及び資源ばかりではなく地球的環境にたち，自然及び資源に対してこれらを積極的に保護し保持に努める．

4.2 社会貢献活動及びボランティア活動の支援

国際企業として事業を行う国の社会貢献活動及びボランティア活動に積極的に参加し，従業員に対してこれらの活動の参加の支援を行う．特に，経済的に恵まれない地域・国に対しては，援助やボランティア活動を集中させる．

4.3 地域社会への積極的な参加

事業を行う国の地域社会の一員，そして良き企業市民として地域社会の行事などには積極的に参加する．参加には従業員や資金ばかりではなく，施設など

citizen, by taking advantage of all managerial resources, including facilities, as well as employees and funds.

4.4 Cooperating with NPOs/NGOs

To cooperate with NPOs and NGOs as appropriate to conduct social contribution or conservative activities of global environment with greater efficiency.

4.5 Promoting Long-term Social Contribution Activities

To integrate long-term, continuous efforts into social contribution and conservative activities of global environment to contribute to the future growth of the country of operation, in addition to efforts in pursuit of quick returns or short-term profits.

あらゆる経営資源を活用する．

4.4 NPO/NGO との連携

より有効な社会貢献，地球環境保全活動などを行うために，NPO/NGO と適宜連携を行う．

4.5 長期的な視野を入れた社会貢献活動の推進

社会貢献，地球環境保全活動などを行う場合には，目先だけの一時的な利益や貢献だけではなく，事業を行う国の将来の発展に寄与するために，長期的計画及び継続的な活動をも視野に入れた社会貢献活動を取り入れる．

参考文献・資料

財団法人経済広報センター編（2005）：企業・団体の危機管理と広報改訂版，財団法人経済広報センター

松下電器産業株式会社（2005）：松下グループ行動基準

General Electric Company (2005): *The Spirit & The Letter*

佐々木力（2004）：箇条書き労働法の実務，中央経済社

谷本寛治（2004）： CSR 経営―企業の社会的責任とステイクホルダー，中央経済社

社団法人日本経済団体連合会（2004）：企業行動憲章　実行の手引き（第 4 版）

水尾順一，田中宏司（2004）： CSR マネジメント―ステークホルダーとの共生と企業の社会的責任，生産性出版

宮田穣（2004）：サステナブル時代のコミュニケーション戦略，同友館

株式会社リコー（2004）：リコーグループ行動規範

労働六法編集委員会編（2004）：労働六法 2004，旬報社

3M Company (2004): *3M Community Giving 2004 Report*

GAP Inc. (2004): *Social Responsibility Report* 2003

ISM (2004): *ISM Principles of Social Responsibility*, Institute for Supply Management, Inc . TM April, 2004

経営倫理実践研究センター監修（2003）：コンプライアンス規定・実践実例集，日本能率協会

株式会社資生堂（2003）： THE SHISEIDO CODE（資生堂企業倫理・行動基準）

日本経団連"社内広報活動のあり方を考える"プロジェクトチーム（2003）：社内広報活動の現状とあり方，日本経済団体連合会・社内広報センター

萩原誠（2003）：広報力が会社を救う，毎日新聞社

松岡三郎，松岡二郎（2003）：口語労働法口語六法全書，自由国民社

Deborah Leipziger (2003): *The Corporate Responsibility code book*, Greenleaf Publishing Ltd.

倉沢進（2002）：コミュニティ論改訂版，放送大学教育振興会

Paine, L.S. (2002): *Value Shift: Why Companies Must Merge Social and Financial Imperatives to Achieve Superior Performance*, McGraw-Hill（鈴木主税，塩原通緒訳『バリューシフト―企業倫理の新時代』毎日新聞社，2004 年）

東京商工会議所編（2001）：図解企業を危機から守る　クライシス・コミュニケーションが見る見るわかる―ケース別チェックテストで「そのとき」に備える 62 項，

サンマーク出版

株式会社ベネッセコーポレーション (2001):ベネッセ企業行動宣言・ベネッセ行動基準

International Labour Organization (2001): *Tripartite Declaration of Principles concerning Multinational Enterprises and Social Policy (Third edition)* (国際労働機関「多国籍企業及び社会政策に関する原則の三者宣言第3版」2001年)

Social Accountability International (2001): SA (Social Accountability) 8000

株式会社ジャパンエナジー (2000):エナジーの創造:購買取引行動指針

Middleberg, D. (2000): *Winning PR in the Wired World: Powerful Communications Strategies for the Noisy, Digital Space*, McGraw-Hill Briefcase Book, McGraw-Hill(茅根知之監修,小原信利訳『インターネット広報戦略:デジタル時代のPR・ブランディング・危機管理』ソフトバンク・パブリッシング,2001年)

Caux Round Table (1994): *Principles For Business* (コー円卓会議「コー円卓会議・企業行動指針」1994年)

山中芳朗,蟻生俊夫 (1990):企業の社会的責任のあり方—企業と地域社会,電力中央研究所報告 Y90005

Carroll, A.B. (1979): *Business & Society: Ethics and Stakeholder Management*, 1st Edition, International Thomson Pub.

その他各種行政法,規制法

賛同組織・団体一覧

本書の出版にあたり、以下の組織・団体から CSR イニシアチブの趣旨及び内容に関してご賛同を頂戴いたしました。ここに記して感謝申し上げます。

  財団法人　関西生産性本部
  社団法人　企業研究会
  NPO 法人　企業社会責任フォーラム
  経営品質協議会
  経営倫理実践研究センター
  財団法人　社会経済生産性本部
  財団法人　人権教育啓発推進センター
  社団法人　全日本能率連盟
  社団法人　中部産業連盟
  日本サプライマネージメント協会
  社団法人　日本消費生活アドバイザー・コンサルタント協会
  麗澤大学企業倫理研究センター
  早稲田大学企業倫理研究所   （50 音順）

＊　　＊　　＊

また、海外の標準化機関へも事前に本書の内容をご覧いただき、感想やアドバイスなどを求めました＊。その結果、限られた時間であったにもかかわらず、次の機関の CSR 担当者から本書の内容や発刊について、よい反応を得ておりますことをここに紹介いたします。
- International Organization for Standardization (ISO)/国際標準化機関
- Standards, Productivity and Innovation Board (SPRING SG)/シンガポール規格協会
- Thai Industrial Standards Institute (TISI)/タイ工業規格協会

なお、上記のほかに本書の内容を提供した海外の標準化機関は次のとおりです。
- American National Standards Institute (ANSI)/米国規格協会
- Associação Brasileira de Normas Técnicas (ABNT)/ブラジル規格協会
- Association Française de Normalisation (AFNOR)/フランス規格協会
- British Standards Institution (BSI)/英国規格協会
- China Association for Standardization (CAS)/中国標準化協会
- Department of Standards Malaysia (DSM)/マレーシア標準局
- Deutsches Institut fur Normung (DIN)/ドイツ規格協会

＊　これらはあくまでも、本書の内容の善し悪しについて検討いただいたもので、ISO 化することについての反応を伺ったものではありません。

- Korean Standards Association (KSA)/韓国標準協会
- Swedish Standards Institute (SIS)/スウェーデン規格協会
- Standards Australia International Ltd (SAI)/オーストラリア規格協会
- Standards Council of Canada (SCC)/カナダ規格評議会
- Standards Institution of Israel (SII)/イスラエル規格協会

CSR イニシアチブ
〜CSR 経営理念・行動憲章・行動基準の推奨モデル〜［英訳付き］
定価：本体 1,400 円（税別）

2005 年 5 月 31 日　第 1 版第 1 刷発行

編　者	水尾　順一・田中　宏司 清水　正道・蟻生　俊夫
監　訳	馬越恵美子・昆　政彦
著　者	日本経営倫理学会・CSR イニシアチブ委員会
発 行 者	坂倉　省吾
発 行 所	財団法人 日本規格協会

権利者との協定により検印省略

〒107-8440　東京都港区赤坂 4 丁目 1-24
http://www.jsa.or.jp/
振替　00160-2-195146

印 刷 所　株式会社平文社
製　　作　有限会社カイ編集舎

© CSR INITIATIVE Committee, 2005　　Printed in Japan
ISBN4-542-70156-5

当会発行図書、海外規格のお求めは、下記をご利用ください。
　カスタマーサービス課：(03)3583-8002
　　書店販売：(03)3583-8041　注文 FAX：(03)3583-0462
編集に関するお問合せは、下記をご利用ください。
　　書籍出版課：(03)3583-8007　　FAX：(03)3582-3372

CSR 関連図書のご案内

[CSR 入門講座 第 1 巻]
CSR の基礎知識

New!

松本恒雄 監修／田中宏司 著

A5 判・130 ページ　　定価 1,365 円（本体 1,300 円）

主要目次
- 第 1 章　CSR とは
- 第 2 章　CSR の具体的な実践活動　〜何をなすべきか〜
- 第 3 章　CSR 推進体制の構築
- 第 4 章　CSR 活動の評価

企業の社会的責任
―求められる新たな経営観―

髙　巖・辻　義信・Scott T. Davis・瀬尾隆史・久保田政一　共著

B6 判・208 ページ　　定価 1,365 円（本体 1,300 円）

主要目次
- 第 1 章　企業の社会的責任（CSR）と企業の役割
- 第 2 章　国際的な動向に見る CSR の現状
- 第 3 章　CSR と欧州連合（EU）
- 第 4 章　社会的責任投資（SRI）の動き
- 第 5 章　わが国経済界の CSR への取組み
- 参考資料編

CSR 企業の社会的責任
事例による企業活動最前線

日本規格協会　編

A5 判・336 ページ　　定価 2,415 円（本体 2,300 円）

主要目次
- 第 1 章　CSR と日本企業の課題
- 第 2 章　わが国企業における CSR 活動
  - 松下電器産業株式会社
  - 株式会社日立製作所
  - ソニー株式会社
  - 富士ゼロックス株式会社
  - 株式会社リコー
  - 三井住友海上火災保険株式会社
  - 株式会社ベネッセコーポレーション
  - スターバックス コーヒー ジャパン 株式会社
  - 株式会社ミツエーリンクス
  - オムロン株式会社
  - 株式会社イトーヨーカ堂
- 第 3 章　社会的責任投資
- 第 4 章　CSR レポート
  - 4.1　環境アニュアルレポート―持続可能な社会に向けて―2003＜抄録＞（日本電気株式会社）
  - 4.2　コーポレート・レスポンシビリティ・レポート 2002＜抄録＞（日本アイ・ビー・エム株式会社）
  - 4.3　GRI サステナビリティ・リポーティング・ガイドライン 2002 日本語版＜抄録＞（GRI）

JSA　日本規格協会　　http://www.jsa.or.jp/